DOWSING

PRACTICAL ENLIGHTENMENT

MAGGIE PERCY
NIGEL PERCY

With gratitude to all the people who have helped us in our dowsing journey

CONTENTS

PREFACE

If you're reading this book, you probably consider yourself to be a spiritual seeker. You're interested in subjects way beyond just the physical realm and everyday existence. In fact, it's probably safe to say, based on all the interactions we've had with people over the years, that spiritual seekers tend to be less attached to the physical realm than the average person, and in many cases, they are uncomfortable in physical form. They wonder how they got here; sometimes they even feel resentful and irritable, wishing to return to another realm that isn't as dirty and filled with pain. The world of energy and spirit calls to them. We have shared that perspective ourselves.

"Enlightenment" seems to be such a spiritual term, something related to heaven and peace and all the things we don't believe we get to experience here on earth. Most spiritual seekers feel drawn to the concept of enlightenment like a magnet, almost like it's a ticket out of here. Yet it isn't entirely clear what enlightenment is. I remember being drawn to the idea of enlightenment when I first started on my spiritual path.

Today as I write this, I feel no more certain of what exactly enlightenment is than I was 20+ years ago. I have become less of a seeker than I was, and more of a person who experiences life and tries to enjoy it. I have stopped feeling I totally do not belong here. In fact, I now feel I don't have to flee the earth and the experience of the physical to be able to experience enlightenment. Somehow, it's in the day-to-day life we all have.

Dowsing has been an amazing help to me in seeing things in new ways, ways that have en-lightened me and made my life happier, healthier and more peaceful. I know I'm not the first person to feel this way. Early in my dowsing career, in the late 90s, I went to a presentation by Joey Korn, where he introduced his book, *Dowsing: A Path To Enlightenment*. I got a copy and read about environmental energies, intention and dowsing, and a whole new world opened to me.

While Joey's book (it really had a powerful effect on me) wasn't really a training on how to become enlightened, the title stuck with me, and over the years I started realizing that dowsing had indeed been a tool for leading me to more enlightened ways of thinking and acting.

Dowsing is a natural skill that allows you to get answers to questions you cannot answer rationally, and in learning to dowse well, I had to make a lot of changes in how I thought and acted. And each of those changes helped create a greater sense of enlightenment in my life. Somehow it's hard to use a natural ability well without becoming more authentic and self-aware, and that leads to a more enlightened viewpoint.

In this book, we want to share with you how the diligent study and practice of dowsing can not only become an amazing tool for extending your intelligence and making your life better. It also helps you develop new ways of thinking, new perspectives and behaviors that naturally funnel you into a more enlightened attitude and approach towards life.

The full benefits of dowsing don't come to those who skim the surface of dowsing or just play at it. Nor does it come to those who arrive at dowsing through the attitude that dowsing is just 'swing a pendulum and make things change', which is more like magic or witchcraft.

You must dive into dowsing with a commitment to become accurate, to use it in your daily life and to look inward for change, not outward. You need to use it in practical ways, not only on airy-fairy stuff that has no impact on your life. Only then will you see the benefits described in this book. We call it 'practical enlightenment' because it isn't some theory or practice you need to be in a convent or hermitage to master. It's the accumulation of daily practice and daily choices that lead you closer and closer to an enlightened attitude and life.

We challenge you to read and apply what we describe here, and then let us know how it has changed your life. Each of us has a unique path. We can't promise exactly how dowsing will create enlightenment in your life. But we'll describe patterns that we have seen to give you some hint of what can come of the daily practice of accurate, practical dowsing.

We don't pretend to be spiritual gurus or saints. We don't even want to be that. We're just ordinary people who have had opportunities to grow because of our love of dowsing, and we look forward to sharing that with you. We hope it opens doors for you as it has for us.

Maggie Percy

January 18, 2015

1

Why Be Enlightened?

What Is Enlightenment?

You hear the word 'enlightenment' and 'enlightened' thrown around a lot in the spiritual and metaphysical world. But what exactly does it mean to you? Can you define it clearly?

I certainly had a feel for what it meant by looking at context, but I have to admit that until I decided to write this book, I would have been hard pressed to define it clearly. So I looked it up. And it didn't really help much. The definitions I found are pretty vague.

Most of us probably have the feeling that being enlightened is somehow better than not being enlightened, but we might have a hard time saying why. References to 'light' abound in the spiritual world. People show their bias by claiming to be 'Lightworkers' and 'of the Light' as if it is obvious that dark things are bad.

So being 'enlightened' is having lots of light and all the good things that go along with it. Sounds like it makes you a more evolved and spiritual person. But in fact how can you tell if you are enlightened?

The word 'aware' comes up frequently as part of the definition of enlightenment. Along the same lines, one thinks of being 'conscious' as opposed to 'un-conscious'. But these are more words that can be rather hard to define. They sound good, but what exactly do they mean, and how does being aware, conscious or enlightened make your life better? What is the difference between conventional awareness and consciousness and spiritual awareness and consciousness? And how can you tell if you are aware and conscious?

Why Care?

Most people in the world would say 'whatever' to enlightenment. Since they don't know what it is, and they have no idea what it can do for them, they don't care. But those of us on a 'spiritual' path have been programmed to regard enlightenment as a good goal. It makes you one of the 'good guys'. It makes you somehow superior to the average human, because not many people are truly enlightened.

Those are pretty lame reasons for pursuing enlightenment. Other than maybe garnering some approval from some people, what good is it? Why bother? Enlightenment doesn't exactly seem that easy to attain, so there should be some powerful motivating factor.

What if being enlightened meant that you became fully self-aware, that you stopped seeing yourself as others do, stopped trying to gain their approval by being what they want, quit following the crowd, really started looking inward and finding out who you are, what your gifts are and why you are here on earth? What if en-lightening yourself was like shining a light into a dark place that you couldn't see and finding out what is there? What if enlightenment meant that a formerly dark and unknown part of you became well-known, fully actualized and fulfilled? What if by becoming enlightened, you had a happier, healthier and more rewarding life?

What is the one universal thing that people want? No, it's not money or fame or even love. They want to be happy. But so often, people think happiness is something outward that they must gain in order to live a joy-filled life. They think being rich will make them happy. Being in a good job will make them happy. Having a family will make them happy. Yet time and again, people get what they've been chasing after, only to find out it doesn't make them happy.

Being happy is an inside job. The process of enlightenment is an inner journey. We believe that as you become more aware, you can become happier. We believe that the path to enlightenment is also the path to happiness and fulfillment. It isn't some vague spiritual goal that gives you brownie points in heaven. It's practical. It's experiential. It's living life to the max.

This book is about enlightenment as a practical concept. Enlightenment as something that, if you achieve it, even bit by bit, your life gets measurably better. We aren't going to be talking a lot about theory, though it will be necessary to discuss it a bit.

Mostly what we want to share is how our journey with the intuitive skill of dowsing has put us on a path to enlightenment. We want to share with you that we didn't engage in dowsing because we thought it would give us enlightenment. We fell in love with dowsing. We were passionate about learning all about it, about becoming masterful at it. That attitude gave us the unwitting tools for allowing the process of enlightenment into our lives: we became passionate, focused, open to change, eager to learn. We committed our time and effort to the process. We weren't expecting overnight success. Little did we know that we were aligning ourselves with a more enlightened existence without even trying.

We know that most people don't have a clear picture of dowsing. For various reasons, they have the wrong idea of what dowsing is. And that means it isn't transforming their lives. They add it on like a bumper sticker you put on your car. They don't use it as a path to enlightenment. And that's ok. It's a choice. But used properly, dowsing is truly a path to enlightenment, a journey of fulfillment that can lead to much happiness. It isn't just understanding dowsing that leads to enlightenment. Nor is it the accurate use of dowsing that gives results. It is your attitude about dowsing that will allow the Universe to give you the gift of enlightenment, step by step, if you allow.

We want to offer you a road map of that journey so that if you choose, you can also use dowsing as a path to your own enlightenment.

WHAT ENLIGHTENMENT IS NOT

We've pointed out that enlightenment is hard to define. You probably are motivated to seek enlightenment, if you are like us. We'd like to point out some of the pitfalls you may encounter on your journey to enlightenment: the one-size-fits-all, instant gratification approaches that are so tempting in situations where you just aren't sure what to do.

As you know, if something sounds too good to be true, it probably is. Enlightenment is not an overnight process. As Malcolm Gladwell pointed out in his book *Outliers*, things can appear to be overnight successes, but rarely are. He was talking about successful artists, inventors and entrepreneurs. He demonstrated that to others, it often seemed successful people went from being unknown and poor one day to rich and successful the next. But that is an illusion. Gladwell makes a convincing argument that on the average, 10,000 hours of hard work went into success.

The same is no doubt true of enlightenment. It's the journey of a lifetime, and at some point, perhaps you reach the destination, and you weren't even aware you arrived. If you are approaching enlightenment as a journey, willing to put in the work and take it step by step, you are bound to become more enlightened. However, if you are eager to reach the destination without putting in the effort, you will be led astray.

Enlightenment is not something you can put on like a new dress. It's not something that happens from the outside in. It isn't about adopting certain behaviors or saying glib phrases.

It isn't enlightenment that has people saying, "It's all good," even when it's bad. It isn't enlightenment that has them squelching their opinions and judgments, as if enlightened people have none.

These poor souls adopt a veneer of what they think is enlightened behavior to cover their natural feelings and attitudes rather than changing them. They are looking for quick fixes that will identify them as enlightened people, but they aren't willing to do the work or put in the time or change their attitudes. By adopting a façade, they become less authentic. And less authentic is less enlightened.

It isn't enlightened to give your power away by seeking the approval of the latest guru. Letting someone else do your thinking is not enlightened. Refusing to question things is not enlightened. True enlightenment can only be attained by asking hard questions and thinking critically. It can only come through being willing to change, to allow change to occur.

Always avoiding conflict is not enlightened behavior. Fear and judgment about conflict will cause you to avoid the necessary pain of evolving as a person, without which you cannot become enlightened.

Becoming passive aggressive because you don't think about and cannot defend your choices is not enlightened. Characterizing yourself as a victim is not enlightened. Truly enlightened people are victors, not victims.

It is an unwelcome fact that human nature works against enlightenment. Even those who recognize they'd like to experience enlightenment face an uphill battle. The desire to reach a goal quickly with as little work as possible is too tempting a proposition for most people. Easier to pretend enlightenment than to become truly enlightened.

The real root of the problem is the low self-esteem most of us have. If we were honest, we'd admit that we think enlightenment is something that only the greatest can aspire to: people like Jesus and Buddha. Not you and I. In believing we cannot succeed, we find it impossible to even try. We settle for the pretense of enlightenment.

True enlightenment is rare, and it doesn't toot its own horn. It is calm and quiet and peaceful. Yet it isn't just cultivating the outward appearance of those things. It's about actually being and reflecting those qualities. How does one go about doing that? In this book, we will point out how our love of dowsing and the pursuit of dowsing excellence gave us a more enlightened outlook as a side effect. It wasn't something we were chasing; it came along the way. And we're still traveling along it.

Is Dowsing The Only Path?

There are many possible paths to enlightenment. And none is superior to the others. You are unique, so your path is yours alone. No one will have the same exact experience you do on your journey. No one can tell you what the best path is for you. It is for you to decide.

For us, dowsing has been a major help in our desire to become more enlightened. But that doesn't mean that it's the path for you. How can you tell if it's for you? It may be for you if you are drawn to dowsing. If you feel passionate about becoming a masterful dowser. Such feelings hint that dowsing may be your route to a more enlightened life. Or maybe it just means you love dowsing.

If you are so passionate about dowsing (or anything, for that matter) that you will commit time and effort to learn all you can about it, to becoming masterful at it; if you are open to changing whatever you must change to become excellent; if you stick with it, then dowsing may well be your path to enlightenment. If you don't feel that way about dowsing, don't feel bad. Keep looking for whatever will inspire you in such a way that you won't give up until you have mastered it.

Dowsing certainly is not for you if you are looking at dowsing as an instant fix, a psychic ability or a magic wand for changing your life without investing any time or effort. That's not what dowsing is, in any case. But that attitude alone is not in alignment with becoming more enlightened. It takes time and effort to grow. If dowsing doesn't make you want to invest in yourself and become better through the use of it, dowsing may not be the path for you.

Don't judge yourself if you aren't sure yet. It takes time for your purpose to unfold and become clear to you. Pursuing what you love is a good thing to do if you desire to become more enlightened, because doing what you don't love has the opposite effect.

As you learn dowsing and practice it, you will be challenged to think in new ways, and that can lead you to enlightenment. Over the years, we've become aware in retrospect how valuable dowsing has been to us for our personal growth and enlightenment. We'd like to share our perspective with you so that you can see how you might use dowsing for the same purpose. Exactly how you go about it and what outcomes you have and how fast it all happens will be unique to you.

2

Dowsing as a Path

WHAT IS DOWSING?

What is dowsing, anyway, and how can it be a path to enlightenment? To answer the second question first, anything can be a path to enlightenment. Dowsing just happened to be it for us. So of course, it's easier for us to draw you a map to enlightenment by using dowsing, because we have some familiarity with that journey.

Until some decades ago, most people only thought of water-witching when they thought about dowsing, if they knew dowsing at all. A select few knew that dowsing could be used to find minerals underground, buried treasure or mundane things like underground cables.

Most dowsers in years past specialized in using dowsing for one purpose only. Water dowsers found water. Those who used dowsing to detect buried cables stuck to that application. The advantage of this was that the dowser only had to learn how to ask one good question or group of related questions. She had time to refine her questions, observe results and tweak technique until she mastered dowsing.

Dowsing is a way of getting answers to questions you cannot answer rationally. In the examples above, basically one question was asked over and over in a variety of circumstances. Where's the water? Of course it seemed magical to the uninitiated, but it also probably seemed a bit boring (unless you were really into finding water!). But all that changed in the 20th century.

"Spiritual dowsing" was born, and dowsing has never been the same since. The earthy water dowsers continued to populate the dowsing organizations like the ASD (American Society of Dowsers). They gathered at monthly chapter meetings and regional conferences. Teaching dowsing was still based on how you used it to find underground water sources.

But a whole new group of people were seeping into the tribe. Hippies and New Agers who believed in yoga and crystal power latched onto dowsing. Dowsing appealed to their interest in psychic, supernatural phenomena. And finding water was just too mundane for them. Some of them realized that since dowsing is a way of answering questions, you can ask any question you like with dowsing. You can ask about your health, your past lives, your chakras or what your frequency is on the Bovis scale.

This proliferation of dowsing applications came with a down side. Suddenly becoming a Master Dowser wasn't just a simple matter of learning how to find water. It wasn't just learning the best single question to ask to find whatever you focused on. Since spiritual dowsers were interested in many subjects, they needed questions for everything. And there weren't mentors to pass workable questions down to them. They were pioneers, and being mostly right-brain dominant, they weren't too eager to analyze and parse the process.

They wanted to do what they did best: connect to their intuition or the Akashic records or whatever it was that knew more than they did. So they simplified dowsing. The process was pared down over and over until finally, all it consisted of was swinging a pendulum and being able to get a 'yes' or a 'no'.

This delighted new generations of dowsers, who were eager to tap into their hidden psychic powers and believed that one could be a full-blown psychic without any work or training. Suddenly everyone was psychic.

Along the way, dowsing still maintained its integrity to some extent. Engineers and scientists who were especially intuitive were drawn to dowsing, and they started to attempt to portray dowsing as a more balanced, scientific discipline. They drew charts, talked about programming and compared the brain waves of dowsers to illustrate the dowsing state. But sadly, even by the 1990s, when I first started dowsing, there were almost no good training manuals for dowsers. *Letter To Robin* by Walt Woods was one of the few simple manuals that actually tried to teach people how to dowse well. And it was good for its time, being one of the few attempts at teaching dowsing to spiritual dowsers, but many years later, it's easy to see how lacking it is.

At the turn of the millennium, dowsing had become a mishmash. Some of the bigger names in dowsing weren't teaching dowsing at all. It was all about using a pendulum like a magic wand, which instead of being a way to get answers, was a way to change anything with intention. The swinging of the pendulum was meant to give it a sense of power, since after all, no one would believe just asking for change by itself would work. So the pendulum, which had always been given way too much power in the dowsing process, became a magic wand instead of a simple tool. Those who followed this method could no longer dowse without a pendulum, since they had been told it was what caused things to change. Welcome to dowsing as a Harry Potter activity!

There was still a small percentage of people who recognized that spiritual dowsing and water dowsing were basically the same technique; asking questions about different things. They realized that dowsing relied on the dowsing state, a good question and trust in the answers. The knew it wasn't about waving a tool around and changing the world, but their approach required even more commitment than asked of water dowsers, because spiritual dowsers had to learn basic dowsing technique and be able to formulate excellent questions about a lot of different subjects. And that didn't come easily to everyone.

In the end, more people wanted to see dowsing as a way to wish your troubles away than as a natural intuitive skill that one could practice and use for improving one's life. It seemed too boring to study technique. Practice was too much effort. And changing yourself or getting answers to mundane questions wasn't as romantic and sexy as doing voodoo on the outside world.

We are among the small percentage of dowsers who define dowsing as it was always defined. Who realize that whether you are looking for water or wanting to know how your chakras are functioning, it's all about asking questions and getting answers. We have found that mastering dowsing depends on being able to use both left and right brain functions. This has the effect of balancing your brain. (And that's a good thing.) Being able to answer questions you cannot answer rationally can be put to all kinds of amazing practical use. It takes the guesswork out of your life and makes life so much better.

We see dowsing as a natural intuitive ability, a skill that can be trained. You can become masterful at dowsing, just as you can master tennis or dance or painting. Skills are things you can discuss, talk about, even argue about. You can theorize the best way to sit a horse or do a certain move in ice skating. This is not an option in religion or magic. We believe that dowsing is a skill. That encourages us to think, to question and to improve what we do. We measure our accuracy and we improve our technique. That is not true of magic, religion or psychic abilities, which is how some people see dowsing. Why is it better that dowsing is seen as a natural skill? When dowsing is seen as a natural skill, it can lead to enlightenment, because only by treating it as a skill will you be put on a journey of personal growth and change, and those things are required for enlightenment.

This book is not a dowsing training. We suggest you consult the Resources at the end of the book if you are interested in becoming a confident, accurate dowser. It is the pursuit of that goal which will take you on a journey of enlightenment, as it did us.

Enlightenment of any kind comes through questing, growth and change, not through un-conscious adherence to dogma you never question and don't understand. We call it 'practical enlightenment', because it starts to benefit you right here in the real world. Dowsing can save you money or make you money. It can help you with your personal growth, finding your life's purpose and healing yourself on all levels. And learning proper dowsing technique will stretch you, challenge you and make you grow. And that growth can lead to a more enlightened existence, as we will explain in later chapters.

Your Journey Is Unique

We can't give you a roadmap to enlightenment through dowsing. You are unique. And the growth you experience as you become a masterful dowser will be different from our path. That is as it should be. In fact, it is part of the wonderful uniqueness of each person's life path and mission.

Remember we said dowsing wasn't a religion? Religions tell you there is one path and only one path to heaven or salvation. They dictate exactly what you must do to achieve it. Dowsing isn't a religion. There are certain basics to learning how to dowse well, but what doors dowsing opens for you will depend on YOU. That's part of the fun of mastering dowsing. It's part of the adventure. It offsets the time, effort and money you invest, rewarding you with unexpected shifts and insights. And over time, those shifts and insights stack up to be huge, powerful and enlightening. And you hadn't really set out with that as your goal. You just wanted to be a good dowser.

Even though your path will be unique to you, just as your fingerprints are, there are some things we can tell you that will perhaps make the journey quicker and smoother for you. You won't have to figure it all out yourself. We're going to share our experiences and insights and offer you some ideas of what the future might hold for you if you commit to mastering dowsing.

We decided we wanted to master dowsing, because we were attracted to it so powerfully we couldn't get enough of it. Along the way, we started seeing other spinoffs, positive things happening that only happened because we were doing our best to learn how to dowse well. These are the things we're going to share with you in this book, so that you will be motivated to continue your dowsing training and practice. Because not only will you become a masterful dowser, you will have a more enlightened existence.

3

Dowsing Technique & Enlightenment

THE DOWSING STATE

It always surprises us how few dowsers are interested in learning how to dowse well. That is because they have been taught that all you need to know is what 'yes' and 'no' mean with your pendulum. It's comforting to think dowsing is that simple, and let's face it, we're all lazy to some extent. Why put forth more effort than necessary?

The sad truth is that most people who think they are dowsing, just because they get a 'yes' or 'no' response with their dowsing tool, are not really dowsing. Because they are not in a dowsing state. They never even heard of the phrase. No one taught them that it is vital to an accurate dowsing answer.

It's very hard to explain and teach about the dowsing state, but it is truly critical to accurate dowsing. If you have not learned to get into a proper dowsing state, you probably are not dowsing. Not only will the dowsing state help you master dowsing; it will introduce you to a more enlightened state of being.

In a similar way to meditation, the dowsing state creates peace and harmony within you while helping you allow the answer you seek to come through. Most people, no matter which side of their brain is dominant, have lots of mental chatter going on in their heads. This 'monkey mind' is counterproductive to getting a good connection so that you can get an accurate dowsing answer.

In our society, the mind is king. The heart is treated as an unreliable poor relation. That's mainly because science has taken precedence over intuition. Science is the religion of the mind. Intuition is the language of the heart. The mind does not naturally wish to give control to the heart. So for most of us, the quiet voice of the heart gets harder to hear as we grow older. Like me, you may get spectacular examples of it breaking through the mental noise, but most of the time, the mind is in the driver's seat.

The mind cannot dowse. The mind must sit down and shut up if you want to dowse well. The mind has its role in dowsing, but the actual dowsing itself requires you to tune intuitively to the answer that comes through your heart. If your world is dominated by your brain, you won't be able to be a good dowser.

On the other hand, those few people who let their heart be in charge may face a different challenge. They don't trust their brain. It seems weak and shallow to them. Yet the brain does have an important role in dowsing.

It is vital to use the rational and intuitive faculties in the appropriate way if you wish to master dowsing. Everyone has a preference for left or right brain. In dowsing, you need to use both sides of your brain appropriately. This is a rare challenge, and accepting it will put you on a path to enlightenment and balance.

The dowsing state itself is not a rational mental activity. So the biggest part of the dowsing state is stopping your normal mental activity and becoming calm and quiet.

Being able to get into a dowsing state puts you in a 'place' where it's easy for the answer to flow to you, naturally. The dowsing state is somewhat like a meditative one, in that your mind is empty. There is no mental chatter or chaos or distraction. But unlike meditation, your mind has one focus. You are laser focused on your dowsing question.

We will discuss the dowsing question later. Most people are not good at forming them, so they only have a vague idea of what they are asking. And their answer reflects that vagueness and lack of focus. We'll talk later about how to form a clear and precise dowsing question, because without that, you have nothing to focus on, and no hope of a meaningful answer.

It has been shown that dowsers who achieve a dowsing state have different brain waves than average people thinking in a normal way. Their brain wave patterns vary from those of monks in meditative states. The dowsing state has been shown scientifically to be unique. It is an altered state, if you will. And you must achieve that altered state if you hope to get accurate answers to your questions.

Meditation is a good practice to help you achieve the dowsing state and quiet your left brain. But you also need to learn to form a clear and precise dowsing question, so that you can focus on that while in a dowsing state.

It is normally accepted that meditation is a path to enlightenment. By learning to achieve the dowsing state, you practice much in the same way as monks do. You learn to detach, relax and empty your mind. You learn to be receptive instead of controlling. For those of us who are left brain dominant, this is heady and scary territory. We aren't used to relinquishing control. We aren't that trusting. So as you begin to master proper dowsing technique, you also begin to let go of control; to relax; to be more in the moment; to detach.

Over time, you start to see changes in how you approach life. It's nearly impossible to be one way while dowsing and the opposite in 'real' life. If you aren't feeling challenged about getting into a dowsing state, you not only are not dowsing, you aren't going to get the full benefits of personal growth it offers. Learning to get into a dowsing state teaches you to adopt attitudes that are beneficial for living a peaceful, balanced life, and that is a major factor in becoming enlightened.

DETACHMENT

Another vital part of mastering dowsing is learning detachment. Detachment is about not being attached to one answer over another. It's ok to prefer one answer over another. But **needing** one answer to be 'right' is attachment, and that leads to problems. That is attachment.

It's important to understand the subtle but real difference between having preferences and being attached. It's kind of like saying there's nothing wrong with owning a big, fancy house. But you don't want it to own you. When you are attached to a particular answer, that attachment will take over the dowsing process and give you the answer you want to hear. The attachment owns you.

You will see this a lot if you try to dowse about a subject that is beyond your level of competence or if you lack detachment. For example, if you dowse on a life and death issue the first month you are a dowser, you probably won't get accurate answers. You need to work up to more challenging topics. And the most challenging topics are the ones you have a strong preference about. Like your dog recovering vs. euthanizing him. Or marrying the person you are infatuated with rather than breaking the engagement because you are fundamentally incompatible.

If you are attached to a certain answer, your dowsing will be inaccurate. Yet the need for detachment is not discussed in most beginner level classes. How can anyone learn to dowse properly without detachment? It's impossible. People who teach detachment try to get you to 'wonder' or be curious about answers. This is a good description of detachment, but it is harder to achieve than you might expect.

When we think back to when we first started dowsing, we remember that it wasn't easy to allow just any answer to come through. The left brain wants to guess the answer. Dowsing is like a test, and and your brain wants to be right. Also, ego jumps in and wants to demonstrate the power of dowsing. We've all seen it. Someone comes up to you without asking and shows off how great their dowsing is at revealing something about you, like whether something is beneficial for you. And you can almost tell that they were going to get that answer no matter what, because they wanted to show off.

It's so tempting to use dowsing to reinforce your prejudices and beliefs. Whether it's beliefs about how vital a certain supplement is or how great a device is for raising your energy, you love having dowsing as 'proof' that you are 'right'. This is ego, not dowsing. You are falling back on this as a substitute for thinking. No one is allowed to question your dowsing, so you feel pretty safe making pronouncements. In cases like this, you lack the necessary detachment for accurate dowsing.

Detachment means you are willing to accept whatever the answer is, even if you don't like it. That level of curiosity is hard to attain. Practice is required. No one masters detachment without practice. And most people don't bother practicing. So their dowsing is false and empty. They rarely, if ever, get wrong answers, because they aren't dowsing. They are using dowsing to support their beliefs and preferences, not to get useful answers to extend their intelligence or change their lives.

You either grow out of this, or you don't. If you decide to master detachment, you learn to let go of judgments and prejudice. It is amazing how that will change your life. Judgment goes along with fear and bias. If you can release judgment, you can be more detached. But those who have strong beliefs and feel that there is only one 'right' way to see the world find that hard to do. If you can overcome the fear of being wrong and the fear of getting an answer you don't want, you definitely will evolve as a person.

I grew up in a very negative and judgmental family. There was only one right way to view things. This made it very hard to learn detachment. Yet I wanted to become a masterful dowser. So I set out to learn curiosity and detachment. I could feel myself flinch and tighten up when I asked questions I was not detached about. It became easier to tell when I was too attached. There was a feeling of constriction that I got which warned me that I was not really detached.

When I felt that way, I learned that my dowsing would not be accurate. It would merely give me the answers I wanted most. So, since I wanted accurate answers, I learned to just let the answers through, no matter whether they were what I wanted or not. It took time and practice, but I got better. I started seeing the world in new ways. One trick that worked for me was to tell myself that I didn't have to act on my dowsing answers if I didn't want to. That seemed to help make it easier to accept a surprising answer.

As I became less attached, I became less judgmental. And at the same time, fear seemed to leave me. If I wasn't regarding one answer as right and another as wrong, it was easier to just allow things to be as they were. Fear was not necessary. I accepted how life was. I came to experience peace more often.

This new attitude allowed me to be more compassionate and accepting of others. Since I wasn't as attached to my beliefs or way of seeing the world, I was less judgmental about others' beliefs. Learning detachment has helped me to create a more peaceful and compassionate lifestyle and outlook, and those are generally accepted as being more enlightened.

Goals & The Dowsing Question

One of the biggest shortcomings we see in most dowsers is their inability to form a good dowsing question. They want to get to the dowsing part, which is what they regard as the most important part of dowsing. To those who are right brain dominant, forming a good dowsing question seems tedious and challenging. They'd much rather grab a pendulum and just get an answer.

We find it hard to convince people of the importance of taking the time to form a good dowsing question. But the fact remains that your dowsing answer is no better than the question you ask. So it behooves you to form a good question.

One of the keys to a good question is knowing exactly what you are asking about. That may sound silly. How could you NOT know what you are asking about? Yet too often, dowsers ask vague and meaningless questions that yield useless answers.

They ask questions like, "Do I need vitamin C?" or "Is this EMF protective device good for me?" or "Is this the best place for me to live?" They feel proud of themselves (and they should) because they are thinking outside the box. They are trying to expand their use of their intuition. But in asking vague questions, they don't get meaningful answers.

Most basic dowsing courses are not that helpful in this regard. They may tell you that you need to ask a good question to get a meaningful answer, but few take the time to show you how to do that. They don't dissect the process. They don't tell you how to add who, what, where, when, how and why to your questions.

A good dowsing question is usually long and detailed. It is necessary to define terms very clearly. Never use vague terms like 'good', 'best' or 'highest good'. They mean little or nothing.

The meanings of words is vital in dowsing; not only what you consciously think they mean, but what your subconscious believes. Sometimes the subconscious does not agree with the conscious mind. If you cut corners when forming dowsing questions and don't define your terms clearly and carefully, you are letting your subconscious run the show. And we all know that the subconscious often has a different agenda from your conscious mind.

It could be argued that forming a good dowsing question is a conscious exercise in deciding what you choose to manifest. You take time to define your terms. That alone is different from the un-conscious living most people do. What do you mean by 'good'? What would give you happiness? How do you measure success? Suddenly you start thinking about what it is you really care about and want to manifest instead of making assumptions and throwing around platitudes.

When we started getting serious about asking good dowsing questions, we realized that we needed to be very clear about our goals before we even started. If we were going to ask about whether to take a job or not, we needed to know what our personal goals were in looking for a job. Otherwise, how could we evaluate the choices?

If we wanted to find the best vet, it was necessary to think very clearly what our values and goals were in terms of a relationship with a vet. These things are individual and unique. You need to spend time making a mental or written list of your goals. Only then can you form a clear dowsing question.

Over the years, as we did this more and more, we began to see how little time we had given in the past to thinking about what our actual goals were. We would do things without really thinking about why. We would try to pick the 'best' accountant without asking ourselves what that meant to us. And we would be disappointed. We would pick a vacation destination from some vague attraction, without asking ourselves what we hoped to experience on the trip, and the outcome was not good. We entered into serious relationships like marriage without contemplating what we considered compatibility to be, and the relationships floundered.

As dowsers, we started to develop a more conscious attitude about creating the outcomes we desired. To do that, we actually gave consideration to what our goals were. We recognized we were unique. We wanted to think about what outcomes we desired rather than letting someone else decide for us. We found it hard at first. But then, over time, it became easier.

This part of dowsing relies on the rational faculty. If you are not strongly left brained, you won't feel comfortable with this, because logic and rationality are not your strong suit. That's ok. Do it anyway. Think of your left brain as having weak muscles, and you are doing sit-ups to make them strong. It gets easier the more you do it.

If you are already left brain dominant, this part of the dowsing process will be easier for you, but you will find the dowsing state a big challenge. Dowsing is a brain balancing activity when done properly, and that leads to all kinds of benefits in your life.

Learning to make a good dowsing question taught us to think about why we were doing what we were doing. It taught us to think about what we intended to create. We began to live a more conscious lifestyle. It became obvious to us that we hadn't really been trying to create anything in particular in the past. Dowsing had taught us to live a more conscious creative lifestyle, thus becoming a vital part of the manifestation process for us. Knowing what you want to manifest and being successful at doing it certainly puts you farther down the path to enlightenment.

TRUSTING Your Intuition

The process of trusting and using your intuition begins with the dowsing state. But it comes into its full power when you get the dowsing answer. At that point, you have a choice. You can trust the answer or not.

Newbies always ask how they can trust their dowsing answers. They ask us how they can be sure the answer is correct; that they didn't just 'make the answer up'. Almost everyone we have taught dowsing has expressed this doubt early in their dowsing career. Both of us went through the exact same same doubts. It's natural.

Remember, we've defined dowsing as getting answers to questions you cannot answer rationally. An answer that you get rationally can be defended. You can look it up. You can 'rationalize' it. Even if you cannot prove it, you can tell people compelling reasons why that answer seems correct to you.

Our left brain dominant culture has taught us to value this process in daily life. People will look askance at you if your reason for a certain answer is, "My heart told me to" or "I dowsed it". You might as well say the fairies told you. It is considered a mental weakness if you cannot support what you say with some type of logical explanation.

So early on, most dowsers are faced with an uncomfortable truth when they get an answer to a question they cannot rationalize. They know in their hearts that most people won't accept how they got the answer, let alone the answer itself. Their natural doubt in their own intuitive abilities and the brainwashing they received in school cause them to question whether the answers are right.

If you don't have good mentoring and support at that stage of your dowsing journey, you soon lose faith and quit dowsing. At least, you don't dowse about anything you expect to take action on. That's because you can't overcome your fear of being wrong and the perception that if you cannot explain your answers, you must have made them up.

The fact is that we all go through this stage. Those of us who master dowsing push through the doubt and keep practicing and learning from good mentors who help us improve our technique and encourage us to dowse about things we can confirm. Being able to see that your dowsing was accurate is vital to trusting your intuition and dowsing.

When I first started dowsing, I didn't have a mentor. So in the books I read, I saw how you can dowse coin tosses or card suits to predict how they'd go. Certainly that is a way of confirming your dowsing. I remember spending one long and tedious evening doing both. First, I think I did the coin tosses. But after many tosses, my prediction rate was still almost 50/50, no better than chance. Discouraged, I switched to card suits, trying to predict which suit would turn up. My success got even worse than mere chance.

The doubting part of my brain told me I must not be very good at dowsing. My results proved that. But then I had an epiphany. I didn't really care that much about the coin tosses and card suits. It was easy to be detached. I really didn't care what the answers were. But I wasn't just detached. I wasn't really interested. I wasn't curious. I was testing myself. That is not the same thing as being detached. I lacked a playful and curious attitude.

To some extent, we have found (and many professional dowsers will agree) that an element of interest or even need is a helpful component when you want to get accurate dowsing results. Dowsing is an intuitive skill, and as with most natural skills, it probably developed to help humans live a safer, even happier, life.

Being secure is a need. You need to be safe. Being happy changes the quality of your life. When dowsing is used for any activity that can improve your life in measurable ways, whether it's finding water to drink or picking the best place to live, it is responding to a need within you to create a better life.

So while you could practice dowsing using anything you can confirm, like coin tosses, you will find that you do better as a rule if you dowse about practical and measurable things that you feel will improve your life. Start with simple things like picking the meal you'd most enjoy off the restaurant menu. Or a place to vacation. As you become more confident, dowse about bigger things, like major life choices involving marriage, career and health.

Dowsing is a way to extend your intelligence. You use your intuition and rational mind to make better decisions than you can make with the rational mind alone. If you dowse about things you can confirm, you will learn to trust your dowsing, your intuition. All masterful dowsers eventually push through that period of doubt. And the only way we know to accomplish it is to dowse more and more about practical, measurable things that matter to you. As you see good results, you will be convinced of the value of dowsing, and you will trust it more and more.

Trusting your dowsing answers will change you. It will stretch you beyond the rational being you have been trained to be. You will add a new dimension to your reality and a new richness to your life experience. You will have a more balanced lifestyle. You will be better connected to your heart. All of these things lead to a more enlightened existence and outlook.

Courage To Act

One of the biggest challenges a dowser faces is accepting that the answers she gets are true. But as hard as that can be, especially when you cannot rationalize them, it is nothing compared to the courage required to act on those answers. The fact is, you are not obliged to act on the dowsing answers you get. Maybe your dowsing indicates that you should not marry John. Or that you need to get a new job in order to be healthy. When your dowsing answers indicate that you need to make a major change in your life, all kinds of fears will be triggered.

You are already a bit fearful, because you cannot adequately explain to anyone why you feel compelled to follow this course of action. You know that if you say you dowsed it, most people will think you have lost your marbles. Then to actually act on that dowsing is even harder. It's like jumping off a cliff and hoping you can fly.

Let me tell you a story. It's one that most people like to hear. Because it's the story of how I listened to my dowsing and changed my life dramatically and found true love with my soul mate. What most people don't know about is the pain, suffering and doubt I went through during the process. The price I paid was huge. I trusted my dowsing, but it nearly killed me. It lost me friends and family. I had to give up my job. I manifested skin cancer and major digestive issues. That isn't going to encourage you to do the same, is it? But the only reason it was so hard on me was because of the beliefs and attitudes I had at the time.

I'll start at the beginning. In the year 2000, after a few years of spiritual seeking, I had embraced t'ai chi, reiki and dowsing. I was quite passionate about becoming a Reiki Master Teacher. And when I was introduced to dowsing in the year 2000 in my Karuna Reiki Master Teacher class, it was like coming home. I had never been so rabidly interested in anything in my life. I took every class, read every book, attended every meeting, joined every group. I couldn't learn enough about dowsing. It combined well with Reiki and opened all kinds of doors for me. Little did I know it had opened the door to a new life.

By May of 2000, my fledgling Reiki practice was faltering, and I couldn't make enough money to do it full time. So I went and got a part time job with a local landscaper.

I felt like a failure. I had put so much effort into my spiritual practice. I had studied and learned and done everything I could to evolve spiritually. I had given up my landscaping company to my business partner and turned to Reiki, but it wasn't sustaining me. I remember in May shaking my fist at heaven and saying, "I just want to make progress spiritually. Meaningful progress. Show me how!" I didn't get an immediate answer, and when I did get the answer, I didn't realize it right away.

In July I joined the Digital Dowsers online email group. At about the same time, I had applied for a job teaching Biology at a local community college. Things started shifting. I got hired as an instructor and started in August. Two weeks prior to that, I had begun a correspondence with someone I met on the dowsing email group. I had written to him that the group seemed to write less about dowsing than other topics, and I wondered if he would be interested in talking with me about dowsing, because his posts seemed intelligent and were mostly about dowsing.

I had no idea who this person was. This was before Facebook, where you see a picture and can read someone's profile information. Nigel Percy was just a name to me. I had no idea of his age, background or marital status. It was purely a dowsing thing.

We began to correspond about dowsing, and my intuition told me that he was meant to be important in my life even beyond dowsing. I did not want to admit that could be true, and I wasn't sure in what way he was meant to be a part of my life. I didn't want to make any big changes. My life was finally coming together. I was married to someone who treated me well. I lived in a nice house, the best I ever lived in, and I had a decent job, even though it wasn't my dream job. I didn't want to make huge, scary changes in my life. In any case, Nigel lived across the ocean in the U.K., and I couldn't see any way that he could be part of my life.

So I tried to ignore the feelings that came through to me as I read the emails about dowsing. I tried to think of ways to fit Nigel Percy into my life as it was. And it didn't work. We had never met in person, and I didn't know anything about him. I couldn't believe I was feeling such a strong conviction that we were meant to be together. I had no interest in upsetting my life so terribly. But one thing I was learning was that I needed to be true to myself. I was surrounded by people who were not true to themselves, and I did not want to end up like them. I started thinking of all the ways I could make Nigel a part of my life without having to change anything big. But in my heart, I knew the powerful attraction I felt would not work well in a 'friend' relationship or long distance while I was married to someone else.

I broached the subject with Nigel of how strangely I felt drawn to him. Some part of me hoped he would laugh it off, or that he was totally happy in his current situation and wouldn't consider making any changes. It turned out he felt the same as I did.

The ensuing 9 or 10 weeks were a blur. Once I admitted that I had to do something, I wasn't sure what it was I needed to do. So I did something I would never recommend to a fledgling dowser. I dowsed about my situation with Nigel. What I dowsed was that he was meant to be my life partner. I then consulted my best friend, who dowsed I would be going to the UK to meet him. I also consulted with a psychic I respected, but she refused to give me advice as to what to do. Instead, she said that no matter what I chose, I could make it a positive outcome.

Sadly, I did not feel that way. My marriage had been eroding for some time, and I had valiantly tried to keep it together. I wasn't being treated badly, but so much was lacking. Things I hadn't really expected to want years before, like having a partner who enjoyed exploring things like metaphysics, healing and animal communication, became really important to my happiness. My spiritual seeking pulled us apart. The differences that had always been there grew, and the time finally came when he looked at me as if I were a witch, because I was doing something that made no sense to him, and he was uncomfortable.

It never occurred to me that my quest for spiritual enlightenment was going to rip my marriage apart. Even though I had known of plenty of couples who split up because only one partner wanted to grow, I never guessed it could happen to me. I suddenly found myself in a very bad position. Everyone was going to judge and blame me if I did what my heart wanted. Furthermore, I had no proof that I was being drawn in a positive direction which would lead to happiness. I had worked so hard all my life to be approved and to fit in, even though I never fit in. And now I felt I was being asked to admit that the person I had tried to be wasn't me after all, and that I was finally going to be authentic. And I knew everyone was going to hate me. And I couldn't even be sure it was worth the risk.

I couldn't reconcile what I felt I needed to do with what others wanted of me. I found myself unable to eat, and my stomach always hurt. I lost weight and couldn't sleep. I tried to share what was going on with my then-husband, hoping something he would say would make it possible to maintain the status quo, but he was not able to discuss things with me. He became angry and threatened by what I said. In retrospect, he made it easier for me by not trying to discuss things with me. His reaction merely convinced me that we had grown too far apart to salvage the relationship. My parents were shocked, and my few close friends became more distant. Almost everyone withdrew their support from me, and I was devastated.

It would have been much easier to just let go of what my dowsing told me to do and follow the wishes of everyone around me. But I had spent my whole life doing that, and it never got me anything. I decided after some weeks of serious consideration that I had to go to the U.K. and meet Nigel. I knew it was the end of my marriage regardless of what happened between us, but I truly believed that my dowsing was correct.

I believed Nigel and I were meant to be life partners. This without ever laying eyes on him.

I put my job and my part time Reiki business on hold. I sat down and talked divorce with my husband. I put my belongings in storage. I was abandoned by all except my little sister, and she was very helpful. My best friend, whom I could have relied on, was still in Canada, as she was a snow bird. And the few other friends I had scattered like leaves on the wind. It was amazing how fast I became a social pariah. But I had the support I needed to get everything done in the time I had.

I don't usually tell the full story of what it took to follow through on my dowsing about Nigel, because it involves so much pain and loss. I went to the U.K. By the time I arrived, I had lost so much weight I was under 100 pounds. My face was ravaged by the removal of two skin cancers. I looked like Frankenstein's monster. But I immediately began to eat and feel better once I arrived there. I knew that was a good sign. I spent 9 months there (an interesting number) and then we returned to the U.S. as husband and wife to begin our life together.

At the time of this writing, we have been married for over 14 years. And it was the best decision I ever made to go meet him in the U.K. It's hard to say what I would have felt if things had not turned out as I had dowsed. But this opportunity showed me where I stood with those closest to me, and how much it all depended on my doing what they wanted. I realized for the first time that no one loved me for me. And that wasn't their fault. I didn't love me for me, so why should they?

I found the courage to act on what I dowsed, and I will be eternally grateful for that. I paid a price, but I will never regret it. The associations I had that fell apart were not real relationships. They were based on me doing what others wanted, not on me being me. Going to the U.K. to meet Nigel was my first action towards learning to love and accept myself as I am. It taught me that being authentic has a price, but that it has many rewards. Perhaps not surprisingly, some family members came around when they saw how much happier and fulfilled I was in my new life.

That one courageous action opened the door to a whole new life for me. Looking back, I realize if I had chickened out, I would still be living as I had before I met Nigel, frustrated and shaking my fist at the sky wondering why the answers I sought never came. Sometimes the resolution of your problem comes in an unexpected package. It can be a challenge to realize what it is. It can take courage to act on it. I realize this is why so few people do this. There are no guarantees of happiness and success. It is always a risk to follow your heart. You have much to lose, but much to gain.

It has been a journey of many years, and I still feel I have a way to go. But following that long ago dowsing led me to be a more authentic person, and doing that has given me more happiness than I can say.

We often share an abbreviated version of this 'how we met' story when we speak at dowsing conferences. People love to hear about soul mates and true love, and we love to show them the benefits of following what you dowse. I am a very private person, though, and I don't like to share my pain and personal life too much. But for this book, it seemed appropriate to give the full story. You can't preach courage to people and act like it's easy. It isn't easy. It may be the right thing to do, but if you are like I was, and you haven't done a lot of self-work (at the time, I had only just begun), following your dowsing can make you ill and cause you to suffer greatly. I allowed others to put guilt on me; I didn't feel I was worthy of being happy and loved; I made an already difficult situation much worse.

Since the year 2000, I have done so much clearing, healing and personal growth work on myself that when I come to a big crossroads, whether it is a decision I must make or just a situation I must deal with, I find it much less challenging to 'do the right thing'. So even though this story, my first story of following my dowsing when it was scary, is one of pain as well as success, don't be frightened. It does get easier. The more authentically you live, the easier it becomes.

I truly believe that when we choose to suppress what matters most to us, we die a little, and the suppressed energy causes imbalance that lead to all kinds of health issues.

If I had stayed in my old situation, I would not have had the gastritis, the weight loss, the skin cancer, the rejection by family and friends. But what would have followed? I would have continued to be the approval-seeking person I always was. I would have suppressed what my real self wanted for fulfillment. I would have compromised. And I believe that would have led to health issues I do not have today. I cannot prove that is the case, but when I look around at all the people I have met who seem to be settling and compromising, it seems reasonable to assume that I would have ended up like them.

Choosing enlightenment is not about choosing ease, comfort and a life on the clouds with the angels. It involves tough choices and sacrifices. It requires change.

It takes courage to follow your dowsing and evolve from a spiritual seeker to one who acts at least somewhat enlightened. For me, following my dowsing has been a good path for getting the answers I sought as a spiritual seeker. The process never ends, but I no longer see myself as just a spiritual seeker. I now see myself as someone who lives a life of greater authenticity and self-awareness, and to me, that is a life which is more enlightened.

4

Summary

WHAT COMES AFTER?

It is said, "before enlightenment, chop wood, carry water; after enlightenment, chop wood, carry water." In focusing on becoming the best dowsers we could be, we found ourselves on the path to enlightenment. We wanted to become more enlightened, but we found that instead of chasing enlightenment, if we just lived life the best way we knew how, enlightened living revealed itself to us in what we did.

There isn't just one path to enlightenment. Do whatever you do with passion and focus. Do the best you can. Keep learning. Keep practicing. Be open to changing how you see the world. The Universe provides you with the opportunities you need to achieve your goals. You don't have to have special training or a fancy guru. Life will provide you with what you need.

Maybe dowsing isn't the path to enlightenment for you. You are a unique individual. For us, dowsing has been a tremendous gateway to more enlightened thinking and living. But enlightenment comes every day in every person or situation you encounter. Enlightenment is an everyday occurrence.

Let the smallest things instruct you. It really is easier than you might expect. It takes time and it takes patience, but the journey is wonderful.

5

Dowsing Opens Doors To Enlightenment

SPINOFFS OF DOWSING

In previous chapters, we've looked at how different aspects of the dowsing process can lead to changes in how you perceive the world. And when that happens, your whole life begins to change.

Dowsing done the correct way, as described in those chapters, becomes a part of your life. It isn't just a tool that you pick up and use now and then when you think you need it, although most people use it that way. In fact, if you are using dowsing that way, you aren't really getting the full benefits. And you may not even be dowsing.

Too often, people use dowsing to confirm what they think is right. They aren't interested in surprising or scary answers. So we like to tell people if you always get the answers you expect, you probably aren't dowsing. Real dowsing leads to surprising answers at times. It leads to scary answers at times. It gives answers that contradict what your rational mind wants to hear.

It's a good sign if this happens occasionally with your dowsing. It's the surprising and scary answers that are the biggest opportunities for you to act courageously and encounter the authentic you.

In this chapter we will share with you some of the big changes we've had thanks to being serious dowsers. I won't promise you will reap these benefits if you are not a serious dowser. But if you are like us, and you take lots of dowsing courses and read dowsing books and dowse a lot and always try to improve your technique and accuracy, and if you think about dowsing and how it has changed your perceptions, you will probably at some point get these benefits. We're hoping that this book can be a catalyst to faster, easier progress for you.

Dowsing is like a lever if you allow it to be. It creates spinoffs by shifting the way you think. You can ignore these spinoffs, but if you are like us, these are the very things you have sought as a spiritually aware person. And being a serious dowser can give you these benefits.

In the following sections, I will show you how dowsing has led us to a more enlightened life by helping us become more authentic, empowered, compassionate, ethical and balanced. If you read the list of the subtitles, I feel certain you will agree that if dowsing can offer you all of these things, you will be a more enlightened person.

CHANGE YOURSELF & Change The World

You've probably heard the famous Gandhi quote:

"Be the change you want to see in the world."

This simple statement seems obvious, but it has great depth and wisdom. Human beings are focused outward most of the time. Humans judge what's 'out there'. If they really don't like it, they try to change it. Whether it's poverty or animal abuse they are fighting, humans feel that in order to experience change, they must impose change on the outer world.

If you see things from Gandhi's perspective, you believe that the best way to change the outer world is to change yourself. At first, this seems ridiculous. How can changing yourself affect poverty or animal abuse? It isn't that changing yourself will eliminate poverty or animal abuse from the planet. Your attitude is based on your perception of reality and 'how things work'. Focusing inward instead of outward is multifaceted.

- You do your best to 'be the change' you want to see in the world. If you want people to treat animals well and respect all life, then you start by doing so yourself.
- As you follow this precept, you will find that it isn't easy to always 'do the right thing'. This gives you the opportunity to learn forgiveness and compassion towards yourself, because you know you are doing your best, and you aren't 100%. That means that nothing is 100%. It allows you to let go of perfectionism.
- As you become more compassionate, you will judge less. You may begin to realize that everyone is doing their best on any given day, even if it does not appear to be so.
- By focusing on changing yourself, you will see that what you fight grows stronger. If you judge yourself as faulty, it's hard to be otherwise. In accepting yourself as perfect as you are, you stop fighting, and that allows you to more easily manifest the outcome you desire.
- By not fighting and judging, you take your power back, because when you are fighting something, you are giving it your power. By taking your power back, you become more empowered. Fighting is not empowering.

Dowsers are not automatically in tune with Gandhi's principle. We have observed many dowsers who have been taught to use dowsing to change their outer world. Even if we defined dowsing as a tool for shifting energies (which we do not), we would be opposed to this outlook. You cannot make meaningful, permanent change in the outer world by trying to force it to align with your values and perception. This attitude is also a violation of free will, which we do not believe is a good practice.

With dowsing, you can pursue a more powerful path by taking responsibility for your life experience. You can become a victor, not a victim. Of course, you can do that without dowsing, but when you dowse in alignment with these values, they have a way of leaching into the fabric of your life. Instead of blaming, complaining and justifying your miserable life, you start seeing yourself as able to make changes. Because in order to make positive change in your life, the only person who must change is you. And you have control over what you choose to do.

Let me share a story with you. Many people will resonate with this situation, as it is one that is quite common. In the final two years of my mother's life, she became our sole responsibility, as my sisters broke off their relationship with her. In their defense, my Mom was not always an easy person to get along with. She was way far along the autistic spectrum. She was brilliant, but she couldn't really carry on a meaningful discussion unless it was about a subject scripted in her mind. Anything that smacked of debate or argument caused her to go haywire.

Frankly, everyone in my family, with the possible exception of one of my sisters, was definitely on the autistic spectrum. But that didn't mean it was easy for us to understand and interact with one another. In her final few years, my Mom, who was a very intelligent and creative person, started to lose her edge mentally. The biggest problem she faced was forgetfulness that grew into a problem she didn't want to admit she had. Like some elderly people who are approaching senility, she became more paranoid than her normal state, and she was a bit paranoid to begin with. When you combine forgetfulness, paranoia and an inability to communicate, you have an explosive mixture.

On top of that, my Mom was very stubborn. And like many elderly people, she didn't want to admit her macular degeneration was ruining her ability to drive; that her osteoporosis made it impossible for her to lift most things over 2 lbs. (even though the doctor told her); that she wasn't really capable of doing her own housework and shopping anymore; that perhaps someone else should help her with her bill paying and finances, because she was too forgetful to keep track. She flat refused to leave the home she had lived in with my Dad for 25 years. But she could simply not take care of herself, and she wouldn't accept much in the way of help. She had gotten to the point that she needed an electric wheelchair to get her mail from the mailbox and a neighbor had to collect and take out her trash, but she still didn't see that as a sign of needing help.

This becomes an excellent example of changing yourself to change the world. I honestly tried to gently persuade my Mom using logic that she needed to make some changes in where and how she lived. But she made it clear she wasn't going to accept any of our suggestions, at least not for long. We were at an impasse. We weren't inclined to try and get her ruled incompetent, because she wasn't. She just was not competent to live the independent lifestyle she had once enjoyed.

We couldn't take away her car keys, nor could we insist she hire a housekeeper or move to assisted living. We presented our case, and then, we let it go. At that point, I realized that unless I changed my perception of the situation, I was going to affect my own health negatively. The stress of worrying what she might do when I could not control her was going to make me ill. I was living 100 miles away, trying to drive to visit, shop and clean for her once a week, bring homemade food and in between, I wondered if she would burn the house down or ruin her finances. I knew I couldn't go on that way.

So for those final few years, I adopted the policy of doing my best (and I sure wasn't 100% at it) to allow my mother to express her free will as much as possible, and control my reaction to her choices, which I didn't always feel were very wise. I did a lot of tapping, The Emotion Code, clearing of beliefs, clearing of chakra links, etc. I used dowsing to determine the best modality for helping me to be at peace with what I couldn't change. I tried to see things from her point of view and have more compassion. I tried to trust and ask for the Universe to protect and help her.

As I became less tense and anxious about her future, I was able to enjoy my time with my Mom a lot more. We still had plenty of 'encounters', but they rarely escalated and never got out of hand, as they had with her and my sisters. My Mom needed me to be there for her. I didn't want to make myself sick over it. I wanted us to have a good relationship and good times together.

The changes I made in myself (in my opinion) led to changes in my Mom. While she didn't immediately accept every suggestion I made, once she realized I wasn't going to push her too hard, she became a bit more open. She was the one who announced out of the blue one day that she was ready to move into assisted living one. She was the one to decide she wanted to go into hospice. There was no way I could ever have forced those things on her, and by giving her the time to choose for herself, I allowed us to have the best possible remaining time together.

It's not that she did everything I wanted. She didn't. She took way longer than I would have liked to make the best decisions. But she made them. And I think if I'd been fighting her and trying to force change on her the whole time, it would have taken longer, and it may have ended up destroying our relationship. Or else, God forbid, the negative things I dwelt on might have manifested.

I'm not saying that I worked on myself to change my beliefs as to what was safest for her. I worked on the emotions and beliefs that said something bad had to happen if she didn't make what I thought was the 'right' decision. I worked on myself to allow her to have free will, even though I didn't think she was making good choices. I worked to let go of the need to prove my attitude was right, and hers was wrong.

As I did this, I saw that on a larger scale, that is all any of us can really do about the world in general. We need to work on how we react to things. It's helpful to accept that this is a free will Universe, whether we like it or not, and that fact will get shoved in our faces over and over until we accept it. The only thing we have control over is ourselves. If we focus dowsing on improving ourselves, we win.

Dowsing that is focused inward, on your own personal growth, will support your spiritual evolution. We have found dowsing to be the most powerful personal growth tool ever. It combines well to enhance the results of any other modality. Dowsing allows you to choose the best method for accomplishing your goals. It can reveal subconscious beliefs that are holding you back. It can guide you to make better choices in career, health, finances and relationships.

Use dowsing as a way to extend your intelligence. By doing so, you enhance your results, no matter what techniques you are using. Dowsing will help you 'know' the best path for your goals. It will also change the way you see the world. That will change your experience of reality.

RELEASE PERFECTIONISM

Modern society has brainwashed us into thinking it's possible to be perfect, while at the same time convincing us we cannot possibly be perfect. Our educational system is largely to blame, though family, cultural and religious values contribute to the confusion.

You learn at a young age that you can get 100% on a test. And that is a perfect score. Although no one ever really claims that 100% on a test means that you know everything there is to know about a subject, nor does it say you learned every single thing the teacher presented in class, there is still the tendency to regard 100% as perfection.

The worst part of this is the implication that perfection is attainable. Because even the best student can't get 100% on every test in every subject. Once we become adults, we intellectually understand this fact. We may have even thought about how some teachers go out of their way to make sure no one gets 100%. We realize no can can know everything. But that 100% looms there as a theoretically attainable goal, one that we sometimes get, and that only makes us feel less perfect.

You may realize that nothing in life is 100% accurate. But somehow, you probably see yourself as defective for not being 100%. You think, "If only

I tried harder," or "If only I were smarter." You set yourself the goal of being 100% when you know it can only lead to disappointment.

Dowsing isn't 100% accurate. Even the best dowsers have less than 100% accuracy. All human endeavors are imperfect. A human cannot be perfect, and what a human does reflects that fact.

We don't promote dowsing as a way to know everything and never make mistakes. We tell people that dowsing will extend your intelligence and help you make a greater percentage of good choices and accurate decisions than if you are using your rational mind alone. This has been the case for us and everyone who dowses the way we do. And we're pretty sure it will work that way for you. But we don't want to give the impression that dowsing is perfect.

It's time to move away from the 'dowsing as psychic ability' perception. The whole perception of psychic abilities is created by conventional folks who think psychic activity is freakish or fake. They act like if someone has a psychic ability, and they are not 100% accurate, then they are charlatans. This is circular reasoning based on their faulty definition and perception of psychic abilities.

We prefer to regard dowsing and other intuitive skills not as psychic, but as latent abilities in most people. Clairvoyance, clairsentience, clairaudience and dowsing can all be trained. They are natural abilities that a small percentage of people have active within them from birth. Most people in our culture have them in latent form, because our culture doesn't value such skills, and most people don't see how they can benefit from them, even if they could tap into them.

When you incorporate intuitive skills with the physical senses and your rational abilities, you have a powerful combination for success. However, it would be wrong to say dowsing or any psychic ability will make you 100% accurate at anything. I learned along the way that my perfectionistic tendencies were actually causing me to make more mistakes. Our friend and colleague Alan Handelsman, who did some sessions with me on this topic, pointed that fact out to me, and it really got me thinking. I became motivated to release perfectionism, and it has made a big difference in my life. I am more relaxed and actually make fewer mistakes.

It was my interest in dowsing and becoming a good dowser that led me to this awareness. I had incorporated an unreasonable desire to be perfect due to the rather stringent academic atmosphere I grew up in. It trained me to feel I always had to try to be 100%, but that I rarely could achieve it. Yet I felt I had to keep trying. It was hard at first when I got answers when dowsing that appeared to be 'wrong'. I hated being wrong. Learning to deal with this and finding ways to use those situations to improve my dowsing led me to see the benefits to be gained from not being 100%. I learned a lot about accurate dowsing through my mistakes. It helped me learn how to teach others to dowse.

Anything can be the catalyst for helping you release the need to be perfect, but for me, it was dowsing. And I will be forever grateful for the more balanced, calm and happy attitude that has bestowed upon me.

Become More Compassionate

I grew up in a very negative and judgmental atmosphere. My family, the religion I was brought up in and my schooling inculcated a very quick-to-judge attitude in me. I tended to judge myself more harshly than I judged others, but I had a very judgmental outlook in general.

I am also a naturally very empathetic person. I find it easy to imagine how others feel. I find it too easy to actually feel what they are feeling. Being naturally empathetic mollified my negative tendencies, but it couldn't cover up the fact that I wasn't really always compassionate. I was aware of how others felt, but it was too easy to think someone could have done better, acted differently, been more honest or helpful. After all, that was how I felt about myself.

Some gurus will say that you cannot love others if you don't love yourself. I believe that is true. For most of my life, I could only see all the defects I had. Every shortcoming seemed huge. Accomplishments seemed to have fleeting value and no residual effect on my life. I was always striving and rarely achieving. At least, that is how it appeared to me. I didn't think much of myself.

Dowsing caused me to release perfectionism. I began to realize no one is perfect, and I am doing my best. And at some point, I began to realize my best was good enough. As I adopted this attitude thanks to dowsing, I began to find it easier to accept the shortcomings of others. I reacted less with judgment and anger and more with compassion.

Dowsing introduced me to the compassionate person I really am. The judgment, fear and negativity had been a layer (albeit thick) over the natural, loving person I really was. As I put aside the attitudes and outlooks that inhibited good dowsing, I became a more authentic, natural human being. I became warmer and quicker to forgive.

You can read about enlightenment and compassion all you like, but actually living it is another story altogether. I always valued compassion, but until my years as a dowser, I didn't find it easy to live compassionately. I believe that's true in part because I was always trying to overlay compassion on top of my natural self-judgment and self-hate. I do believe it's impossible to really be compassionate with others when you hate or judge yourself. By helping me to release self-judgment and to be kinder to myself, dowsing helped me to be more compassionate to others.

Be Authentic

We love dowsing, and we are aware that at best, it is a fringe activity. Like many other metaphysical and spiritual interests, dowsing is something people tend to keep to themselves, because they don't want to be judged or lampooned.

While there is a contingent in the dowsing community of people who don't give a darn about what anyone thinks of them, most dowsers tend to be concerned about how their families and friends regard them. Even those who are not classic people-pleasers tend to avoid confrontation, so they keep their opinions and activities to themselves or only share with like-minded people. One of the things that keeps dowsing unaccepted is that so many people feel it is unacceptable.

If you are participating in an activity that family and friends would regard as freakish or blasphemy, you are being authentic in spite of outside pressure. How much you reveal is a sign of how authentic you feel you can safely be. This is a personal choice and depends on your goals. If it's really important that people like you, you won't show them you are doing something they disagree with or fear. If harmony is your priority, you may not mention dowsing in front of your spouse, if you are sure he/she will ridicule it or become angry.

If you love dowsing, but you are afraid to do it in public or admit you are a dowser, you are also afraid of being authentically you. This reluctance is a sign that you are equating being authentic with taking risks, being rejected or being judged.

When I started dowsing, I had already gotten my Reiki Master Teacher training. I had some training in animal communication, and I'd been practicing T'ai Chi Chih. These were activities that made my heart sing. I felt alive when I was doing them. I loved learning about them. I enjoyed doing them well. And I especially celebrated how much positive change they brought to my life.

I had a fast learning curve in energy techniques and metaphysics, and by the time I encountered dowsing in my Karuna Reiki Master Teacher training, I was already getting some raised eyebrows at home and among family and friends. I was so excited, I didn't really register what that meant until one day my Mom took my then-husband aside and said, "You make sure she doesn't go too far down this road." From that point, the two of them were more obviously against me practicing the things I was interested in. Although the details were never discussed, it seemed to me a religious stand on their parts, because both had fundamental type religious outlooks, and they had begun to regard me as a sort of witch.

A close friend whom I helped overcome a problem by using animal communication began to look at me sideways. Pretty soon, the majority of people in direct contact with me were either neutral or negative about my extracurricular interests and activities. I only had acceptance in the classes and groups I participated in. I really only had one person in my life, my best friend (who was quite new in my life) who was totally supportive of my interests. The weight of being judged became a burden. I was faced with a choice. I could be authentically me, or I could be what others wanted me to be.

If I chose the former, they would reject and censure me. If I chose to please them, I would surely become resentful of giving up the few things I felt passionate about. In the end for me, it wasn't consciously about choosing to be authentic. It's just that I knew I would become bitter, resentful and probably ill if I did what they wanted, and I couldn't face a future like that. I had gotten a taste of what living my passion was about, and I couldn't voluntarily give it up.

In choosing dowsing and my other interests, I lost a lot of people and a lot of approval. But I embraced the authentic me, and although it was very hard to do, it felt right and it felt good. I am so grateful that dowsing provided the springboard for me to launch to a whole new level of living. I had been going through life as a Stepford wife, and I was finally free to be me.

What dowsing helped me to face was the fact that I had been hiding my true feelings, my desires and my reactions for years. I had done my best to be a 'good daughter', 'good employee', 'good wife' and 'good friend' based on what I thought others wanted and would value. I remember saying when I was in my twenties that I was a chameleon. I could blend in anywhere and get along with most anyone if I tried. It seemed to be a facility with many benefits. But the down side was that in trying to please so many different people, I lost track of who I really was.

I would tell myself I was happy, but I wasn't. I would tell myself I wasn't that stressed, but I was. I said I was healthy, because I was healthier than people with awful diseases, but I wasn't as healthy as I could be or as I wanted to be. I had buried my own dreams and preferences for so long that I didn't really know what I wanted. My life was nothing more than a series of tasks. I was trying to do as much as I could as well as I could to be considered a good person. But I wasn't authentic. I wasn't even aware of who the authentic me was.

I doubt most people find that dowsing is the door to authenticity. But it can be. If you find the courage to be open (not preachy) about your dowsing, the chips will fall where they may. People who love you for yourself will hang around. Those who only appreciate you for doing what they want will move out of your life. I personally don't see how that is a bad thing, though it can be a very painful transition.

For me, dowsing opened the door to being authentically me. I had to admit that I was not a mainstream person. I finally admitted that I was different from others, and that wasn't a bad thing. I learned to release fear of rejection, the need for approval, the tendency I had to hide my light under a bushel. Dowsing encouraged me to discover and become who I really am. It is one of the best journeys I have ever taken, and while dowsing isn't the only way to achieve authenticity, it certainly is one option.

I guarantee that being authentic may be challenging and even painful at times, but you will be happier, healthier and more fulfilled and at peace if you do your best to express your authentic self. Being authentically you is definitely a more enlightened lifestyle.

Develop **Self-Awareness**

According to Wikipedia: '*Self-awareness is the capacity for introspection and the ability to recognize oneself as an individual separate from the environment and other individuals. It is not to be confused with consciousness. While consciousness is being aware of one's environment and body and lifestyle, self-awareness is the recognition of that consciousness.'*

Self-awareness is an aspect of being fully enlightened. Being conscious and then self-aware shifts your perception of reality. So much of the 'programming' of modern society is to domesticate and homogenize the individual. If you are 'different', you don't fit in. If you value things that others do not, you are a freak. If you have a passion others cannot understand, you are shunned. Love, approval and support in a society depend on your behavior. And the best behavior, the most rewarded behavior, is to be like everyone else. This totally contradicts self-awareness.

Religious programming trains you to look outward, to feel defective and to avoid doing anything that could be judged as 'selfish'. So in addition to cultural programming, your individuality is worn down and smoothed out by religion.

Layer upon layer of similar programming by political groups, hobby groups and interest groups further erode your ability to recognize yourself as unique, much less to value being different. It's almost as if all the structures of society are aimed at removing self-awareness as much as possible.

Far from being wrong, a sense of self is necessary for a balanced, meaningful life. I remember as a child, I was taught not to ask for anything. In fact, I was rewarded for keeping my mouth shut and not asking for things. Still, as a very young girl, I had some powerful dreams and desires. I remember when I was maybe 4, going on 5, I finally got the courage up to ask my folks for a pony. I had been thinking about it forever. I had it all figured out. We could keep the pony in our fenced back yard (we had a small house on a small lot in the suburbs, and of course it wasn't zoned for livestock); I would feed him; I would brush him; I could ride him the back yard. I was too young then to have the big picture. It was something I wanted so much, I was willing to actually ask. Of course the answer was 'no', and rightly so.

But it taught me not to ask. I found it easier not to ask for toys and such. Why risk disappointment? Besides, my parents bragged that I didn't ask for things, and their approval was not easily won. I didn't ask to go to the circus even once, although it came to our area every year. I really wanted to go and see the animals. But I knew my parents had no interest in it, and by then, I realized we didn't have enough money for such frivolity.

By the time I was 12, I had learned to bury my dreams. I understood it was best not to share them with anyone, as they would never happen anyway. It hurts to bury your desires, so I learned not to think about them, not to feel anything about them. Pretty soon, I was able to become a proper, programmable student and employee. I got high marks on both counts, wherever I went. But I wasn't really me. I didn't even want to think about me. I just wanted to be considered good enough.

Like me, you won't want to be self-aware if that means discovering how different you are from others and how the things you value seem odd to them. If self-awareness ultimately leads to rejection, what's the benefit? Better to keep your head down and plow on through life.

In order to become a masterful dowser, I had to start becoming more authentic and aware. I had to have clear goals, know how I felt about something and be able to form good questions about choices. I had to be honest with myself and look inward. As I began to change myself, I realized I had to know myself to change myself or to evolve as a person. Self-awareness came with a price, but it opened doors to a new way of thinking. It made it easier for me to think more carefully and ask questions about things. I began to be able to express my own opinions and values clearly. Where previously, I merely parroted what I had been taught to believe, now I actually thought things through. In doing so, I realized that my true values were not always in alignment with those I had been programmed to adopt.

Becoming more self-aware led me to a more authentic lifestyle. Becoming more authentic aided greater self-awareness. It became easier to understand my purpose being here on earth. And that gave my life greater meaning and joy. There are many ways that you can become self-aware, but for me, dowsing played a major role, thus leading me to a more enlightened life.

Love Yourself

It can be very challenging to become aware of the authentic 'you'. This is especially true if you have the belief that the real you is not lovable, as most of us do. There are many reasons for this pervasive and persistent untruth.

Some religious upbringing brainwashes you into thinking you are flawed and sinful at birth. The educational system may not have been geared to acknowledge your brand of intelligence, and you may have come to feel stupid as a result. Your parents treated you the way their parents treated them, even though when they were children, they didn't really like how they were treated. By the time you become an adult, you wouldn't know unconditional love if it came up and hugged you.

People who are interested in 'fringe' subjects have an additional strike against them. Conventional society judges anyone who is interested in psychic or unexplained activity. They are freakish. They are stupid. They are gullible.

For this reason, many dowsing enthusiasts or those who are simply curious about dowsing hide their passion or interest from friends and family, believing (or knowing) that admitting an interest in something so 'incredible' will lose them points or even lead to rejection. It can be hard for many people to take a pendulum out in public, especially for those who are introverts. Dowsing becomes for them a clandestine activity like drinking on the sly, with many of the same fears attached to it.

My family did not embrace dowsing or energy work, even though I was very passionate about it. I didn't try to persuade them to my way of thinking, but I also didn't hide everything I believed or did. The more candid I was, the more people looked at me like I was a witch. It all seemed so rational to me, to be interested in the mind-body-spirit connection and the development of focused intuition through dowsing. I sensed that there was distance growing in my relationships, but I was so captivated by what I was learning that I assumed they would all eventually catch up with me, and at least accept me for who I was. Or maybe even just be happy that I was happy.

You see, that was what was happening. I had discovered something I had a passion for. I was immersing myself in learning about it and practicing it. For the first time in my life, I was throwing myself into something 100% and really loving it. Reiki and dowsing and other techniques spoke to a part of me that just 'knew' what's important and how things work. I couldn't articulate it, but it was like finding a missing piece of myself, and the dirty looks of family or friends were not going to stop me from following such a rewarding path.

When you find something you love doing and you choose to do it to the best of your ability, you are meeting and nourishing your true self. You are giving yourself permission to be you. And that is the best way to love yourself. When you deny what you most love, you are rejecting yourself. Because what you most love is your real mission on earth. Denying your authentic self almost guarantees you won't accomplish your life's purpose.

There are fears and risks involved in loving yourself. When you embrace your passion, whatever it is, you may see relationships crumble. Anyone close to you who does not love himself or herself will not be comfortable around you if you have the courage to love and nourish yourself. The energy mismatch is just too great.

I lost many friends and had a falling out with many family members when I chose to follow my true path and do what I loved. When I decided that living my passion was important, I was saying I had a right to be selfish. I chose to love myself as I was. I no longer was willing to be another person just to gain the approval of people. The authentic me came out, and after decades of hiding that person, there was hell to pay.

Since everyone's situation is unique, I can't predict what would happen if you started really loving yourself and living a life that is true to the real you. But I ended up divorced, rejected by my Mom, and I lost some friends, one whom I had thought really cared about me.

The thing is, people can't stand it when you prove their belief system is wrong. Even if you aren't asking them to change, you are an unpleasant reminder of how they have sold out, and it makes them unhappy and uncomfortable, so much so that they strike out at you. They have to judge you to prove to themselves that not being authentic is the way to be.

Loving yourself is a sure way to separate your real friends and loved ones from those who are sleepwalking. For many years, I was surrounded by people like me, who thought very little of themselves and never went out of their way to find their passion and live life in a way they loved. When I gave that role up and got to know what I really wanted, and I embraced that and filled my heart with joy, it was too much for them. I had no idea I would have to give them up, but like attracts like, and we were no longer sharing the same values or outlook on life.

If you go from trying to be what others want to being yourself and loving who you are, your outer world is bound to shift. How much and in what way is hard to predict. A lot depends on how big a shift it is. For me, it was huge. And it had huge consequences. For you, it might be less. But for almost everyone, learning to really love who you are is a big enough shift that if you can make it, your world will never be the same. And that is a good thing.

We have pointed out in previous chapters that if you don't really know yourself, you can't really love yourself. And if you can't really love yourself, you can't love others. Learning to love yourself as you are is the beginning of unconditional love. You can't hate yourself and love others. Loving unconditionally is a goal of most major religions. Real unconditional love is an aspect of being enlightened. If you love unconditionally, you are living a more enlightened life.

Dowsing isn't the only way to learn to value and love yourself. But for me, it was the catalyst and the path to accepting myself and feeling good about myself and not caring so much about what others thought. If you are one of the lucky ones, it will help you see that you are a lovable person and introduce you to the practice of unconditional love.

Know Your Purpose

Many spiritual seekers are caught up in the quest to discover their life's purpose. I can remember for most of my life, I felt a bit lost. I thought there should be some sense of having chosen the right path, of having an awareness of a larger purpose to my life, but instead, it seemed my life drifted, bouncing off this or that and then changing direction, never having a beacon to follow or a conviction of a mission. I tried many different careers and had a variety of hobbies and interests I pursued, but none 'called' me. That is, until I got involved in Reiki and dowsing.

I was introduced to Reiki in the late 90s and to dowsing at the beginning of 2000. I felt a magnetic attraction for these subjects, and I plunged into them with a passion, yet I couldn't figure out what I was meant to do with them. I consulted a psychic yearly, and one of my favorite questions over the years was, "What am I meant to be doing with my life?" One psychic said I was meant to be a teacher. Another told me I was a counselor. I was chagrined, because I wanted to be told I was a born healer. It certainly seemed a bit shinier than teacher or counselor.

There are some fallacies in this approach. Asking someone else to tell you your life's purpose doesn't really make sense. You should know yourself better than anyone. Needing someone to tell you is a sign that you probably aren't too familiar with the authentic you. Or that if you have gotten a glimpse, you are not loving what you are seeing. That was the state I was in when I went to psychics. I didn't know myself. I had such a thick layer of denial and judgment smothering the authentic me that I couldn't begin to figure out what to do with myself. I couldn't bear the thought of disapproval from those I loved.

Because dowsing became a path to discovering my authentic self and learning to love myself more, it helped me to come closer to understanding and embracing my life's purpose. I admitted that I was meant to do something with dowsing beyond making it a nice hobby. I accepted that my mission would distance me from my family and dissolve certain relationships, but it also attracted new ones that were deeper and more fulfilling.

Obviously you have your own unique mission. Maybe your life's purpose doesn't involve having to break up relationships. If not, you are lucky. My path was one of being thrown out into the cruel world without much support, because if I hadn't been, I would have stayed cocooned in the bosom of my family and never done anything risky or unconventional, and that would have been a shame. I needed to be rejected so I could find myself and my purpose. Those who rejected me did me the biggest favor they could have. It forced me to change, to become more independent and less approval-seeking. That led to me becoming accepting of the person I really am, which led to enjoying my life more, because I was doing what I loved.

What if your life's purpose is to enjoy life? What if it isn't necessary for you to give up the things you love most? What if doing what you love IS your life's purpose? Dowsing helped me to see that I can't compare my mission to anyone else's. I'm not Mother Teresa. I'm not Gandhi. My life is a success if I feel fulfilled doing what I do. I have no need to compare to others or to have the stamp of approval of others.

Dowsing has been my path to this realization. It has been liberating. No longer do I strive trying to discover my life's purpose. I just live the best life I can, doing what I love most. To me, that seems a more enlightened approach to life.

CREATE PEACE & Harmony

There's a lot of talk in the spiritual community about peace and harmony being so important, but it seems to me that there's precious little of both.

Drama and struggle is as rampant among spiritual seekers as it is in the conventional world. Oh, many don't want to admit it. It seems the default setting for New Agers is, "It's all good," even when it's bad. I have met so many 'spiritual' people who are a bundle of anger and frustration with a thin layer of goodwill on top. When the veneer cracks, it isn't pretty.

The Law of Attraction tells us that you can't fake how you feel. Your vibrational frequency isn't what you want it to be. It's what you are. If you fail to do the self-work to release the negative feelings and to shift the judgmental and dualistic attitude, no amount of "It's all good" is going to get you enlightenment. Suppressing negative feelings is not a solution, yet many people do this instead of self-work.

If you value peace and harmony and want to experience them, you must be at peace and harmonious. You can't fake it. I was never a very peaceful and harmonious person. I had a demeanor that was not prone to wide mood swings. I prided myself in that. I tried very hard to be a good and pleasant person. But I wasn't happy. I wasn't authentic. I didn't love myself.

The path to inner peace is the same path to being authentic, loving yourself and finding your purpose in life. It creates peace when you do those things. Not just striving for them; doing them.

There are many modalities that help you make changes that can lead to inner peace. We have used many of them. We suggest you do daily self-work using whatever method allows you to see the shifts we've described in earlier chapters. Dowsing is a wonderful tool to have on this journey. It can help you pick the most effective method for your goals. Since you are unique, your path will be your own. We can't tell you exactly what to do, but dowsing certainly was a big help in creating a more peaceful, harmonious atmosphere in our lives.

Sometimes the way to a destination isn't the straight road you expect. For me, it was important to make peace and harmony a choice, but achieving it was not a simple step-by-step, linear process. In fact, it seemed that they were out of reach when I tried to go straight for them. On the other hand, when I chose to focus on being more authentic and loving myself, peace and harmony were natural rewards along the way. My dowsing journey taught me these things, and I will be forever grateful.

There are other circuitous windings on the dowsing journey that in the end deliver unexpected treasures. Those treasures are best left as side effects instead of goals. Too many dowsers are attracted to dowsing because they perceive it as a quick way to become powerful. Dowsing is marketed as a psychic activity, and as such, appears to be easy to do. If dowsing appeals to you mainly for the power it gives, you can end up in trouble. If you can even get power without lots of hard work, it would not change your life for the better, because if you haven't transformed your victim energy and your anger and other negative emotions, getting power will only turn you into a victimizer.

This is another example of why working on yourself is the best priority. And learning to be an accurate dowser is a great goal. Along the way, as you will see in later sections, you will find you have enhanced intuition, at times almost like being psychic. But that is not the goal of becoming a dowser. It is a pleasant perk that comes to those who take the indirect path. They don't hunger for power; they don't cling to power; they don't feel tempted to abuse power. It just is.

It has been an unexpected lesson to me on my dowsing journey that some of the best rewards are those that I haven't even tried to achieve. Peace and harmony are more a part of my daily life than they ever were, thanks to dowsing.

Trust Yourself & The Universe

One of the biggest stumbling blocks everyone faces when they begin to dowse is trust. The most common question we get from new dowsers is, "How do I know I'm not making the answers up?" This relates to trust. And trust grows out of confidence. There are a number of reasons most dowsers never progress beyond this doubting phase. If you find yourself stuck here, there are some things you can do:

- **Dowse about things you can confirm.** We don't mean coin tosses and card suits. They are meaningless. Instead, dowse about things that matter, but not too much. Like whether it will rain today, so you know whether to carry an umbrella, or what item on the restaurant menu you will most enjoy. Every time you dowse about something that you can confirm, your confidence will grow. *Please note: Using dowsing to confirm your dowsing answers is not a valid method.*

- **Don't expect dowsing to be 100% right.** There are many reasons for dowsing error: lack of practice, poor or inadequate technique (like bad questions or not being in a dowsing state), polarity reversal, attachment to a particular answer, etc. All of these things can be minimized with training and practice. But the truth is that no human activity is 100%. Even the best dowsers get the wrong answer from time to time. Dowsing is not a psychic activity in the way you might think of it. You think of psychics as people blessed with a gift that they didn't have to train. They just have it. Dowsing is a skill. You must train and practice to become accurate. And even then, you will make mistakes. The important thing to remember is that dowsing makes you more accurate overall in the choices you make in life. Without dowsing, you'd be guessing. Dowsing takes the guesswork out of your life.

- **Build a solid foundation in terms of your understanding of what dowsing is.** Too many new dowsers don't really know what dowsing is. That inhibits trust. Blind faith is not the same as trust. Dowsing isn't a religion. You don't have to take everything on faith. There are many good books, courses and meetings you can attend to broaden your understanding of what dowsing is. Knowledge will allow you to have more trust. It won't seem like blind faith anymore. Any dowsing guru who preaches about dowsing things that cannot be verified is asking you to take it on faith. Dowsing unverifiable subjects is NOT a good topic for new dowsers. Avoid it.

What about when you have done all of the above, but you still find yourself doubting your answers? Give yourself time. Be patient. This is probably a manifestation of your own self-doubt, not just doubt about dowsing. If you have a tendency to be a perfectionist, dowsing may seem like going out on a limb. Talk to yourself. Understand that you were going to make a choice anyway, and without dowsing, it would have been pure guesswork. (Remember, you only dowse about things you cannot know rationally.)

Therefore, regardless of whether your dowsing is accurate, it is still better than simply guessing. When you realize this, you can see that what dowsing does is increase your accuracy overall in life. It doesn't promise 100% accuracy. It just promises that if you dowse the right way, you will make more accurate choices than if you didn't dowse at all. This should please the perfectionist in you. Dowsing helps you become more accurate.

It's possible that your doubt also relates to deep-seated lack of faith in yourself. You may not be a perfectionist. Maybe you were just verbally abused your whole childhood about how dumb or worthless you were. If you decide to become a dowser, you will have to face your own trust issues. The biggest trust issue to overcome is to trust yourself. This is where self-work comes in handy. Use whatever modality you like to release negative emotions and shift faulty beliefs about yourself and the world. As you shift, you trust more. Dowsing is a great motivator that way.

Lastly, trusting the Universe can be hard. The Universe often is seen in our minds as a parallel to our earthly parents. Your parents were human, so they weren't perfect. You will project all your parent issues onto the Universe. If your parents didn't support you in some fashion, whether financially or emotionally, you will expect the same treatment from the Universe.

When you are dowsing, you often are asked to take action without any guarantee that things will turn out the way you wish. Your trust issues with the Universe will pop. You'll start thinking, "If I do this, how do I know that things will turn out better?" Because you are not totally in control of events, you will worry that the Universe isn't going to step up and deliver.

This is another opportunity for self-work. The Universe is not your parents. It gives you unconditional love and support. Learn the Law of Attraction and release your doubts and mistrust of the Universe. Stop thinking of God as your father. It will activate all kinds of issues, unless your parents were perfect, which I'm pretty sure they were not. Doing the self-work, as always, brings you closer to an enlightened state, as you discard baggage that was dragging you down.

When you get a dowsing answer, and you are certain you have used the best dowsing technique possible, act on it. If the subject you were dowsing about is critical, get outside dowsing aid. Consult a dowsing professional or get a dowsing buddy to blind dowse for you. It's always wise to get a second opinion on any major life choice. Trust your dowsing, but don't be foolish.

Developing trust in your dowsing simply is a matter of trusting your dowsing, which means trusting yourself and the Universe as well as your dowsing technique. By following the suggestions in this chapter, you will find that you learn to trust your dowsing, but beyond that, you will also become more enlightened, because trusting that life is proceeding according to plan is part of an enlightened outlook.

Become Empowered

We've suggested in earlier chapters that you not chase power as a goal in dowsing. Rather, think of dowsing as a tool that will help you 'step into your power' naturally. That's a New Age phrase that is hard to define, isn't it? All this talk of empowerment sounds good, but you may find it rather difficult to figure out how to become empowered. So let's examine it more carefully.

Empowerment is part of self-awareness. Most humans are not very self-aware. For one thing, they've been taught that it's selfish to focus on yourself, to do for yourself, to want anything for your self, even to want to be happy. Also, most humans are running on autopilot, with the subconscious running the show. To become self-aware, you need to become more conscious, and you need to release any judgment against doing for yourself. These are both harder to achieve than you might think, and they usually require long-term self-work. (There that concept is again: you need to work on changing yourself to change your life experience.)

Dowsing can give you the wonderful spinoff of empowerment. To become more empowered, you must learn to see life differently and to live differently. Empowerment cannot be magically conferred upon you, even though it is a natural human tendency to wish this could be so. I can remember being a little disappointed after each Reiki attunement I received. I was not conscious that I was a better healer afterwards. I felt pretty much the same. I realized I had hoped for some magical process to flick a switch so I could be a miraculous Reiki healer. It didn't happen that way, and it doesn't happen that way with dowsing, either.

Don't chase power through dowsing. You don't need to, and in any case, the direct route is fraught with pitfalls. Seek to become an accurate dowser and change your life. As you succeed, you will become more authentic. You will learn your life's purpose. You will begin to trust yourself and the Universe more.

Empowerment is a side effect of this process. If you trust your dowsing and follow it and improve your life, you will begin to turn inward when you have a decision to make. You will believe that you are capable of choosing well. You will tend to stop looking for outside approval for everything you do. This is 'taking your power back', because when you seek approval, you give others the right to criticize and manipulate you for their own ends. Acting that way says you aren't as qualified as they are to make the decisions in your life.

Don't get me wrong: sometimes you need outside help. But you know if you're the kind of person who always vacillates about making a choice. You know if you are always doubting your own ability to 'do the right thing'. You know if you are a people-pleaser or addicted to going to psychics for advice. As we have shown in earlier chapters, the process of learning to dowse the right way can lead to increased confidence and trust in yourself and the Universe. That will naturally empower you to feel more comfortable making choices that in the past would have sent you scurrying for help.

An aspect of empowerment that is usually reserved for advanced training is that of personal responsibility. Personal responsibility is often seen as 'blame' by many spiritual seekers. Those who are trapped in victim mode and feel powerless do not have and do not want personal responsibility. To them, it sounds like they're just going to be buried in more negativity and blame if they choose to be responsible.

Often in public dowsing forums, I have been criticized for saying people are co-creators of their reality, that they are in charge of their life experience. In every case, those who disagreed with me believed people are powerless victims.

Everyone is entitled to choose their perception of reality. But if you are a dowser, you need to step beyond this limiting victim mentality that is so prevalent on earth. In doing so, you draw closer to enlightenment.

You cannot ever master dowsing if you cling to victimhood. If you think life happens to you, you'll never have the mindset to become a good dowser. If you are a masterful dowser, you are capable of improving your life on a daily basis. You believe that improvement is in YOUR hands with dowsing. That you can make better choices that lead to greater health and well-being. You no longer see yourself as a powerless victim.

This is what empowerment really is. It isn't about having power over others at all. It isn't about being equal to others. It's not about having the things other people have or the opportunities they have. Empowerment is about knowing that you are the pilot of your life, not the passenger. You aren't the pilot of anyone else's life, just your own. And that is enough. That is empowerment. We are all capable of becoming empowered, but few rise to the challenge. Dowsing can be an excellent path to empowerment if you commit to being a masterful dowser.

Bᴇ Ethical

I think it's fair to say there is no one on earth who has the desire to be unethical in what they do. Ethics are like integrity; everyone wants to think they are on the right side of that subject. But how can you be sure you are ethical?

Because dowsing is a powerful technique, it can be abused. Therefore, it is necessary to have a code of dowsing ethics so that you don't stray from appropriate dowsing practices. A code of ethics provides guidelines that allow you to make wise choices about your dowsing.

It's important to make the distinction here and now between the concept of ethics and 'doing good'. The two are not the same. In the dowsing community at this time, there are a lot of people who speak about using dowsing 'for good' or 'only for the highest good". Those are highfalutin' words, but what exactly do they mean?

While ethics can be highly personal, good intentions are far moreso. What I consider to be a worthy or 'good' application of dowsing might shock someone else. Pleading good intentions as rationalization for actions doesn't buy points in court or in life. As they say, "the road to hell is paved with good intentions". This saying is a reminder that good intentions don't always have a good outcome. That you need something more than personal prejudice in order to be on the side of the angels, so to speak.

This is where ethics come in. A code of ethics can be personal, but it also can be part of an agreement among a group of people. While good intentions are always in your head, and no one else can know or prove them, ethics are something that sit outside of your mind. They are guidelines that you can compare your actions to, so as to make sure you are behaving in an appropriate fashion. These guidelines allow people to have meaningful discussions about a variety of situations and come to an agreement about what ethical behavior is.

Here is an example of the difference: a code of ethics at the workplace might say you cannot accept gifts from parties who are doing business with the company, because they could be construed as bribes. Someone who goes only by good intentions would say, if a person accepts a bribe, it's bad, but if it's an innocent gift, it's ok. The problem here is there is no outside source able to tell what's what. The person accepting the gift may be innocent, but the gift could still be meant as a bribe and later used for leverage. When you start trying to know what goes on in people's minds, you rapidly lose credibility, because no one can prove anything. This is especially true if you are trying to rationalize your behavior by saying you had good intentions.

A code of ethics allows you to have guidelines that are the same for everyone. Everyone is held to the same standard. Anyone can examine their own or other's behavior based on the code and know if they are in compliance or not. There is no need to argue intentions, which cannot be proven in any case.

No doubt the world would be a better place if each human being was able to create their own code of ethics and live by them without interference. But that's never going to happen, so having a code agreed upon by a group of people is the next best thing. There isn't a code of ethics in dowsing as far as I can see at this time. There's plenty of talk about 'good works', which won't be defined the same by everyone. There is too much reliance on 'intention'.

Let me tell you a story about good intentions and how it can lead you astray.

In my first several months of being a dowser, healer and energy worker, I was approached by a very good friend who was worried about her daughter. The daughter had two young children and was going through a bitter, drawn-out divorce with a husband who supposedly used drugs and was a lawyer. He knew every trick in the book for delaying the divorce, and it had dragged on forever. Finally, the daughter had found a decent job, but it required her to move to another location. She was unable to do that until the soon-to-be-ex signed a document, which he hadn't. In fact, he had not signed a document by the deadline even once during the proceedings. He always managed to get an extension.

She was desperate not to lose this job, and it meant he had to sign the document on time. My friend asked could I help make that happen? I was new to dowsing and energy work. I had taken many courses and read some books. I wasn't sure I could help, but it felt like it was a worthy cause. So I said I would try. I thought that asking that the energy between everyone be harmonious and cooperative would do the trick. My dowsing indicated that he was not inclined to sign on time. So I asked if his High Self would give permission for me to harmonize his energy and help him be cooperative. I got 'yes'. I then used intention to shift the energy into a harmonious pattern.

He signed the document right away, then went back to being a real bastard. Of course, I was thrilled he signed the document, as that was important for my friend's daughter. But when I saw he went right back to being a jerk, I realized that what I had done was to override his free will. I realized that I used the High Self ploy to get the 'yes' answer I wanted so I could do what I felt was 'the right thing'. I meddled in his energy without his real permission. I got results, but in a way, it scared me. Because I'm smart enough to know this: if a newbie like me can make someone do something against their will (right or wrong), then it is possible in general. And that means someone could do it to me or someone I love, and they might not always be doing something 'good'. Or they might think it's 'good', but it is a violation of my privacy and free will.

I admit some part of me didn't mind that I forced that jerk to do the right thing. But a bigger part of me saw I was playing God. I was deciding what was right. I had only heard one side of the story. I was old enough to know that in divorces, there are often things said which are exaggerations or outright lies. I'm not saying my friend or her daughter lied, but their perceptions certainly were prejudiced. While the ex probably was a total jerk, it wasn't my place to judge him or try to change him without his permission.

One of the easiest ways to test your dowsing ethics is to ask if what you espouse were turned on you, how would you feel? Would you be comfortable having someone force you to do something you didn't consciously want to do, even if it was for your own or the greater good? Do you feel that someone else's opinion about what is right is more valid than yours and should be imposed on you?

Another way of looking at this is beyond the logical fact that if something is ok for you to do, it's ok for others to do, there is the question of karma. No one likes to accumulate bad karma. If you invade someone's privacy or rob them of free will, sooner or later, the same will be done to you. So do as you would have others do unto you.

We have a firm code of dowsing ethics. It's really quite simple. Don't dowse for or about anyone without their expressed verbal or written permission. No cheating by asking their High Self or some other source you can't prove gave you the permission. No vague "May I? Can I? Should I?"

No one doubts the good intentions of dowsers. But dowsing is such a powerful tool, that it must be used with restraint. We never want to violate the privacy or free will of another. Even if we wish we could persuade them to change. Dowsing has helped me to differentiate between the vagueness of good intentions and the clarity of a code of ethics. Living by a code of ethics shows that you respect others and that you intend to use your power wisely and well. These are certainly signs of enlightenment.

· · ·

Respect Free Will

Free will is pretty tricky. Whenever there are opposing views, there will be conflicts about the exercise of free will. It's important to respect free will. It's especially important to respect the free will of those with whom you disagree. It's easy to celebrate the freedom of choice of those who think like you.

Free will is much like free speech in that if you rob another of that freedom, you are robbing yourself. You cannot have laws that limit the freedom to speak your mind, because then you start judging what is worthy of being spoken, and there is never 100% agreement on that. It is vital to uphold the rights of others to express an opposing view to yours. That guarantees that your right to express yourself will continue.

How does this relate to dowsing? Dowsing is powerful. Governments have the power to enact laws to limit behaviors and the exercise of free will. Dowsing is an individual practice that has no checks and balances (other than karma), and thus is actually more dangerous than political power.

An unethical dowser or energy worker can attempt to transform other people and places without their permission, just because she is judgmental or afraid of what they are doing. Spiritual or energetic vigilanteism is an expression of fear and ego. It is not enlightened behavior to judge or act on fear. It is not enlightened behavior to rob others of free will. Yet that is what some dowsing gurus are preaching to their flock.

If you have a noisy neighbor or disagree with a politician, there are dowsing gurus who say it's ok to dowse about them or even try to change them without permission. Recently in a Radionics group I belong to on Facebook, someone posted that he had obtained some personal trash from a neighbor who had done something he judged was wrong. For six months he did radionics work to punish that neighbor. He was pleased to report the neighbor had just been evicted, and the way he said it, you could tell he was taking responsibility for this event and was gleeful about it. I made a comment about how that seemed a bit like practicing voodoo, and he had the nerve to say I should save my preaching for church; that radionics was essentially sorcery. Why was I interested in it if I wasn't willing to use it?

Radionics is not dowsing, but it is very like the false dowsing method being preached by some dowsing gurus. They have combined intention and dowsing and now define dowsing as a healing or transformation method. It is worrying to think that dowsing is headed in the direction of this radionics example. People need ethics to keep them in check when they have power. If someone has enough fear or anger, and they have no code of ethics, sooner or later they will violate the free will of someone.

Ethical dowsing teaches you to respect free will. It forces you to release fear, because otherwise it just isn't easy to be ethical. Being afraid that others can impact your life negatively is a very disempowered position. It says that others are more powerful than you are, and that you cannot choose your life. It becomes very enlightening to learn to release fear and realize that you do have more choice than you realized in manifesting the life you want.

Denying others free will is also tantamount to denying yourself free will. If there is any justification for taking away the free will of someone using dowsing, then that says anyone is entitled to rob you of free will or attempt to change you or violate your privacy without your permission.

In helping to show you the value of respecting free will, in causing you to become less fearful and take responsibility for your life, dowsing can be a tremendous boost in your enlightenment process.

Live In The Now

Living in the 'now' is universally seen as being 'better' and more enlightened than dwelling in the past or the future. Focusing on the past robs you of the joy that living in the present offers. Focusing on the future creates anxiety about things you cannot control. Being fully present pulls all your energy into one place and helps you be more powerful.

When I first started dowsing, I was like a lot of people. I was eager to use it to predict the future. I soon found that future dowsing was less reliable than dowsing present time things. I feel certain that much of the inaccuracy was due to fear. It is never wise to dowse about anything you have strong emotions about. If you are anxious about a future possibility, you shouldn't dowse about it. If you are attached to a particular answer (and if you dowse about the future, it's almost always true that you want one answer over another), you are asking for bad results.

In the many years I have been dowsing, I have had some excellent future dowsing results. But I have also had many inaccurate future dowsing answers. We'll tell you to avoid dowsing the future, especially if you care about the answer. But you know what? Go ahead and do it and prove to yourself that it's mostly a waste of time. That is the best way to convince yourself not to dowse about the distant future.

I am a recovering perfectionist who has a tendency to desire control. Dowsing seemed to me an excellent way to give me what I wanted. I could predict the future and avoid making mistakes. But it didn't work out that way. My dowsing was unreliable, and I soon learned to take it with a grain of salt. Whereas present dowsing was quite reliable for me, future dowsing was a bit of a mess.

This forced me to face up to my personality and what it said about me and what it was doing to me. I had to admit I was being a bit controlling, that I didn't trust things would work out, and that I was playing to fear and anxiety. So I made a commitment to stop doing those things. I realized that trusting the Universe would be a good thing, as would loving myself as I was. I started using methods I knew so I could shift the energy and see things differently. I began to see myself as more perfect, just as I was. It is a journey, and it takes time, but I am getting there. Trusting the Universe that my future would work out ok was harder than I thought. It revealed a lot of beliefs and traumas related to my family and parents. I discovered I was seeing the Universe as my parents, and with all their faults. This is obviously silly, so I began to do the work to shift that perception.

When I say 'future dowsing' I am not including dowsing that lists my goals and helps me make a choice that will give better outcomes in the future. I am talking more about dowsing like a psychic activity.

If I hadn't been wanting to be an accurate dowser, I wouldn't have cared. I would have continued to dowse the future a lot. I would have kept being the person I was, mistrusting the Universe and wanting control so I could feel perfect. Dowsing helped highlight those tendencies, giving me a chance to change them. I'm glad I did.

Don't judge yourself in situations like this. Don't feel wrong for who you are. But if your outlook is making you anxious and not helping you, the way mine was, then changing it makes sense. Most of the time you are dowsing about the future, you are not in present moment fully. You are anxious about what might happen, desiring to control it. Give yourself a chance to become more enlightened and live in the 'now'.

Past dowsing can be equally limiting. Dowsing will allow you to discover about past lives, if that is your belief system. Too many people have false impressions about what past lives are and how they affect us. While it is true that other lifetimes can have an effect on this one, it is a mistake to spend too much time dwelling on your past lives. It is a tempting and intriguing thing to dowse about when you first learn to dowse, but doing so can activate connections to other lives that are not beneficial.

Spending your dowsing time on your present is good, as what you are dowsing about, you are focusing on. Focusing on the present is a way of gathering your power. There are many gurus who preach about the value of being in the 'now'. Choosing to do that with your dowsing will give you all the benefits of that choice, which is a very enlightened condition.

. . .

Enhanced Intelligence Through **Intuition**

It is self-evident that dowsing, being a way of getting answers to questions you cannot answer rationally, extends your intelligence through the use of focused intuition. Because it is focused, you don't have to wait around for intuitive 'hits'. You can ask specific questions and get answers.

So much stress in life is because you just don't know the answers. There is so much guesswork. Should you go to the doctor for your kid's symptoms? Are those supplements worth the investment? Will you enjoy going to a specific resort in Jamaica for vacation this August? You just aren't sure. You cannot know rationally. Yet, if you knew the answers, life would be easier. You could reduce stress, knowing that you were doing the best thing for your goals.

Dowsing gives you answers to questions like these, reducing stress and helping you make better choices. But it also extends your intelligence. It is perhaps arguable that being more intelligent is not necessarily being more enlightened. But I am of the opinion that greater intelligence allows for greater flexibility, and that is going to allow you to be more enlightened.

The practice of dowsing, done the right way, reveals things to you that you never would have guessed. The surprising dowsing answers are a challenge to see life in a different way. If you are dowsing properly, a certain percentage of your dowsing answers will not be as you expected. And what you do then is going to give you an opportunity to become more enlightened.

If your dowsing response is unexpected, you can just ignore it. You can rationalize that it was wrong. If you do that, you won't change, and you won't see growth. The unexpected answers are asking you to see things in new ways. If you examine those answers and shift your perception, you will find yourself becoming more enlightened.

Personal growth is a journey towards enlightenment. Never changing your opinion is a refusal to grow. Dowsing is one of the many ways life will challenge you to see things in new ways. It's far gentler than some methods. You can still say no, but why not give things a chance?

We all have the chance to learn every day until the day we die. We only stop learning if we choose to. Clinging to dogma of one kind or another stops growth. And that halts your progress towards enlightenment. Embrace the surprising answers you sometimes get with dowsing and see where they lead you.

Over the years, the world has become bigger and more complex as our dowsing has revealed things we never would have guessed. We believe in the invisible world of energies. We recognize the huge impact they have on our lives. We have discovered many mechanisms for change and healing, and we have seen them work.

Dowsing has helped us to realize that everything is energy, and that addressing energy can lead to change. We've learned a lot about the power of intention and how to enhance it. You can learn all these lessons in other ways as well. Dowsing isn't the only path to a more enlightened view of reality. But it is the one that has done the most for us.

Enhancing All Your Intuitive Abilities

We've found that dowsing has enhanced all our intuitive abilities. This won't be the case for all dowsers. Those who dowse with a tool have a tendency to block out all information coming in except the movement of the tool. This will limit or prevent other intuitive messages from coming through.

That's why we like to dowse without a tool. When dowsing devicelessly, you can allow the answer to come in and be aware of any other information that comes through. Maybe you see a vision, or hear a word, or get a feeling. How your other abilities grow will depend on how you dowse and what talents you favor. So it isn't easy to describe the path, because it will vary.

As the Buddhists say, don't seek psychic powers on the path to enlightenment. They come as a side effect. We don't want you to become a seeker of psychic abilities. But we can report that proper dowsing technique will enhance your other intuitive senses over time, and that is basically what your natural psychic abilities are.

I am not naturally clairvoyant. Yet, since I began to dowse, I have become much more visual intuitively. I now get glimpses of pictures when dowsing about energies at a location. I never was able to do that in the past. It's as if by focusing on getting answers, you are asking for information to come through, and it will come through in other ways in addition to the 'yes' or 'no' response to your question.

As you become more advanced as a dowser, you will find that you are able to know what the answer is before your tool indicates it. You will find yourself aware that you don't need to dowse about some things. You already know the answers, even if they are not rational answers. And you feel confident about them.

When you reach this point, you are becoming more intuitive and living the way humans were intended to live, with dowsing and intuition integrated into life, not something you tack on. It may not be considered enlightened to live a fully intuitive life, but we feel that doing so will usually lead to a more enlightened existence. If you listen to your heart, which you must do in order to be intuitive, you will be more in tune with life. You will be happier. You will be more fulfilled. How can that be anything but enlightening?

QUESTION EVERYTHING

Dowsing the right way will challenge you to think more critically. By that, we mean you will question things more. You will define terms more clearly. You will think about your goals. You will want to find out for yourself about things rather than just be told what to believe or do.

This process leads to greater self-awareness. You will be choosing consciously to do the things that matter to you. You will be seeking information for creating a happy, healthy life. This is the total opposite of parking yourself in front of a TV and being programmed.

As you become more self-aware and think critically, you will start to question more things. While this will not endear you to those who want followers who are sheep, it will help you to avoid un-conscious living and poor choices. You may end up questioning your religious faith or your political affiliation. You may begin to wonder about the ethics of the company you work for.

You will also question your own motives. You will want to become more authentic and live in accord with your values.

As you go through this process, you will discover most people do not value your ability to think. They will feel threatened and offended by your attitude. Most people prefer to be sheep. They want a guru to tell them what to believe and do. If you question their dearly held beliefs, they will attack you or they will not want to be around you.

This can be particularly unpleasant if your family and close friends reject you. While it is not desirable to ask questions purely to stir up trouble, it is worthwhile to be yourself. If close friends and family do not like your asking questions, then they are not comfortable with the real you. They may not be supportive of the authentic you. They may even be afraid of who you are.

You will have to make choices along the way. Questioning everything does not mean you have a mission to persuade others to think like you do, or even to think critically themselves. Learning to accept that not all people are like you, and that most do not want to think is an important step on the path to enlightenment.

You don't need everyone to think like you in order to be enlightened yourself. You aren't responsible for saving the world. It's ok if people reject your point of view or approach to life. You don't have to change to win their approval, and they don't have to change to win yours. You may not feel like hanging out with people who think you shouldn't question things, but you don't have to judge or fear them.

We think it's great to think. And we see it as part of a more enlightened viewpoint. But that doesn't mean everyone is going to value it or strive for it. You will be judged for thinking critically. You will be rejected at times. Don't give it up because of that. Forgive people. You weren't always this way, and one day, they may feel differently. Until then, they are a part of this perfect Universe just as they are.

RESOURCES

Resources

Books

We're written many books for dowsers. If you are new to dowsing, get our course in a book, entitled *Learn Dowsing: Your Natural Psychic Power.* We've written over 20 books on dowsing and related topics which can be found at all major online retailers of books.

PLEASE LEAVE A REVIEW

When we were first learning to dowse, there weren't many books for dowsers. If you enjoyed this book, please leave a review wherever you purchased it, because that will help us reach more dowsers and help them master this powerful skill.

ABOUT THE AUTHORS

Maggie and Nigel Percy met online in 2000 through their mutual love of dowsing. They spent the next 20+ years serving a global clientele with dowsing and energy clearing methods. During that time, they presented at many conferences, created the online Dowsing World Summit and gave free dowsing training through videos and articles on their websites. They've written over 20 books on dowsing and metaphysical topics and have published fiction using the pen names Maggie McPhee and Andrew Elgin. To see all their books, visit your favorite online retailer.

www.ingramcontent.com/pod-product-compliance
Lightning Source LLC
LaVergne TN
LVHW051704080426
835511LV00017B/2718